Artists' Impressions in

Artists' Impressions in Architectural Design

Bob Giddings
Margaret Horne

SPON PRESS
Taylor & Francis Group

London and New York

First published 2002
by Spon Press
11 New Fetter Lane, London EC4P 4EE

Simultaneously published in the USA and Canada
by Spon Press
29 West 35th Street, New York, NY 10001

Spon Press is an imprint of the Taylor & Francis Group

Typeset in Arial by M Rules
Printed and bound in Malta by
Gutenberg Press Ltd

British Library Cataloguing in Publication Data
A catalogue record for this book is available from the British Library

Library of Congress Cataloging in Publication Data
Giddings, Bob, 1952–
    Artists' impressions in architectural design / Bob Giddings and
    Margaret Horne.
        p.   cm.
    Includes bibliographical references and index.
    1. Architecture – Designs and plans – Presentation drawings. 2.
    Architectural rendering – Technique. 3. Architectural drawing –
    technique. I. Horne, Margaret, 1948– II. Title
NA2714.G53 2001
720'.28'4 – dc21   2001041080

ISBN 0-419-26200 8 (hbk)
ISBN 0-419-23600-7 (pbk)

Contents

Acknowledgements

The authors would like to thank the following individuals and organizations for their help during the preparation of this book.

Alan Bridges: Alan Davidson: Alan Day: Alison Greig: Andrea Christelis: Andrew Carothers: Andrew Roberts: Angela Giral: Ayssar Arida: B.J. Novitski: Bauke de Vries: Brian Hutchings: Bob Stone: Carl Laubin: Catherine Raftgou: Chris Emmerson: Christian Groothuizen: Cindy Wasserman: David Chang: Clare Endicott: Deborah Kirschner: Don Kelman: Elizabeth Walker: Evelyne Trehin: Fleur Castell: George Saumarez-Smith: Glenn Goldman: Graham Cook: Howard Wolff: Hugh Whitehead: Ian Hamilton: Jamal Abed: Jamie Scowcroft: James Akers: James Brogan: Jane Tobin: Jemma Crowhurst: Jo Hammond: Jo Wisdom: John Marx: John Stuart Pryce: Justin Shigemi: Katy Harris: Keith Mendenhall: Keith Schmidt: K.C. Kwok: Kristine Fallon: Laura Parker: Laurence Bain: Lawrence Eaton: Lawrence Hughes: Lee Dunnette: Lionel Fanshawe: Lucy Francis: Margo Stipe: Mark Arthur: Mark Martin: Marian Bozdoc: Martin Stancliffe: Meg Whittle: Mick Brundle: Mig Halpine: Mikki Carpenter: Nabil Gholam: Neil Bingham: Neil Spiller: Neil Taylor: Nicholas Weingarten: Nick Browning: Nicky Dewe: Norma Aubertin-Potter: Paul Richens: Peter McGuckin: Peter Stocker: Peter Trowles: Pierre el Khoury: Rebecca Harrison: Rob Becker: Romaine Govett: Sally Kennedy: Sarah Rutt: Simone Poulton: Steve McIntyre: Susan Palmer: Thomas D Grischkowsky: Tina Wilson: Tom Schaller: Varant Alexandrian: Winnie Tyrrell.

American University of Beirut Library: Arup Associates: Association for Computer-Aided Design in Architecture: Autodesk, Inc.: Avery Architectural and Fine Arts Library, Columbia University in the City of New York: Bartlett School of Architecture, University College London: Bentley Systems Inc: Bibliothèque Nationale Institut de France: British Architectural Library, Drawings Collection, Royal Institute of British Architects: British Library: Building Design Partnership: Centre for Advanced Studies in Architecture, University of Bath: Cesar Pelli & Associates Inc.: Codrington Library, All Souls College, Oxford: Construction Industry Computing Association: Derek Lovejoy Partnership: Eindhoven University of Technology: Erith and Terry: FaulknerBrowns: Fondation Le Corbusier: Form 4 Architects: Foster and Partners: Frank Lloyd Wright Foundation: Frank O Gehry & Associates: Glasgow City Council, Cultural and Leisure Services: Glasgow School of Art: Hardy Holzman Pfeiffer Associates: Hayes Davidson: Ian Ritchie Architects: Insite Environments: Jeremy Dixon — Edward Jones: Kristine Fallon Associates, Inc.: Library, St Paul's Cathedral: London Borough of Lambeth, Archives Department: MacCormac Jamieson Pritchard: Martin Centre, University of Cambridge: Metropolitan Cathedral of Christ the King, Liverpool: Michael Hopkins and Partners: Michael Wilford and Partners: MUSE Virtual Presence: Museum of Modern Art, New York: Nabil Gholam: Nicholas Grimshaw & Partners: Ricardo Bofill: Richard Rogers Partnership: Robinson Library, University of Newcastle upon Tyne: School of Architecture, New Jersey Institute of Technology: Skidmore Owings and Merrill: Sir John Soane's Museum: Terry Farrell and Partners: University of California, Berkeley: University of Northumbria at Newcastle Library: YRM.

Chapter 1 Context and Introduction

The design for a building begins with a concept, an idea in the mind of the architect. This image must be conveyed to clients, who understandably need to know what their building will look like. It needs to be communicated to planning authorities and perhaps to committees judging competitions or organizing exhibitions. Members of the public also have an interest in finding out what is planned for their neighbourhood. The architectural intention of a design often needs to be communicated to people who may or may not possess architectural understanding. It is not normally practical to create a prototype building, nor is it sufficient to describe the inspiration of the architect in words. A visual representation is required. Presentation techniques, for different stages of the design process, have ranged from the brief conceptual sketch, geometrical plan, section and elevation, picturesque perspective, physical scale model through to today's computer simulation. Thoughts are represented either subjectively, providing an *impression* of the building, or objectively, via precise geometry attempting to define the building in advance, the two approaches perhaps reflecting that architecture belongs to both art and science. Some worthy presentation drawings and models, whether for realized projects or not, have found their way into galleries, archives, collections and books, and as such have become publications, moving outside the building process and into the cultural institutions of architecture (Lipstadt 1989). Whatever the form of the *artist's impression*, its importance and interest, and debate on its effectiveness, cannot relate solely to the representation itself. We must take into account the process by which it came into being. The visual representation of buildings has taken many forms, and its rich history, great diversity and fascinating future remain as interesting today as ever.

Artists' Impressions are drawings and models of designs for a building that does not exist at the time of their preparation. It can be difficult to differentiate between this type and representations of completed buildings that are known as topographical depictions (Stamp 1982). The position of *architect as artist,* within the background of British architecture, was arguably the historical position and held good until building activity in the 20th century started to gain pace. Prior to the 13th century an important church may have had a simple plan, usually based on an existing building, but construction could continue over several centuries during which time styles changed and drawings did not survive. If a drawing was used it could be very large, or even full size, prepared on tracing boards or on specially prepared plaster screed floors (Porter 1997). In the Gothic period (12th to 16th century), although the geometry was sophisticated, architecture was fundamentally a *constructive practice*, operating through well-established traditions and geometric rules, discussed and applied directly on site. Art was *applied* to buildings, in the form of marble statues, alabaster images, stained glass, English embroidery, and curvilinear mouldings. The 14th century saw more architectural ideas conceived as geometric representations, and window tracery adopted both flowing patterns and rectilinear forms. However it was the period of the Renaissance (16th to 19th century) and the introduction of new scientific discoveries, including geometrical theory and practical systems for making perspectives, that signalled a milestone in the representation of architecture. Due to its distance from Italy, England was not influenced by the movement until a century after its birth in Florence, when it became fashionable for young men to visit Italy and return with Renaissance ideas. Creative influences

also developed as many artists and craftsmen were displaced, perhaps for political or religious reasons, from important artistic centres in Europe, and sought refuge in England. Various English monarchs who had liked concepts they had seen in Europe also introduced artistic fashions and trends. However during the 17th century the designers of buildings were mostly working masters who had risen from the rank of mason, carpenter or bricklayer. It was the 18th century that saw the emergence of architects who had begun their careers as artists or sculptors, often studying in Italy. Architects began to engage pupils and the profession of architecture began to be consolidated. Towards the end of the 18th century the Picturesque Tradition, and its fashion for architecture and landscape gardening, saw an establishment of designs composed as pictures. The new media and techniques of the Renaissance had resulted in greater freedom of expression for the draughtsman and increased stature for the artist. Drawings, paintings and physical models, making use of the technique of perspective, were used as a way of presenting ideas to clients, and some beautiful presentations emerged.

The 19th century witnessed a period of great innovation. It brought the invention and development of various new aids for architectural drawing (Hambly 1982). These ranged from accurate, sophisticated mathematical instruments such as the elliptograph, pantograph and scale rule, to the simpler tee square, drawing board and tracing paper. Hambly (1982) described how a new type of instrument-maker emerged in Britain to meet the demand from engineering, architectural and surveying professions. W. F. Stanley started his business in 1853 and invented and produced a wide range of drawing instruments that were technically efficient and simple for the draughtsman to use. His business survived for over one hundred years.

Photography was also born in the mid-19th century, and various photographic processes developed as the technology improved. The technique of photomontage, superimposing designs of proposed buildings onto photographs of existing scenes, was introduced in an attempt to provide a new realism. Yet photography could never portray a building that did not exist – *one of the few situations in which the camera is not an option* (Myerscough-Walker 1958), but it was welcomed by architects as an important aid for the visualization of existing buildings. Photography offered an alternative to sketching, in the recording of existing details, but the simplicity and portability of the sketchbook were features that stood the test of time. The latter part of the 19th century was a period when visual art was of great significance. Architects with sufficient means travelled regularly to the continent with pocket-sized sketchbooks to record architectural details. Some celebrated artist–architects emerged at this time, with artistic style varying from soft-edged watercolour impressions to exploration of pen and pencil techniques and aerial views. The representation of depth in a two dimensional medium resulted in concern for shadows, and renderings aimed for a geometrical accuracy in their production. At the end of the 19th century the formation of societies such as the Art-Workers Guild (1884) and the Arts and Craft Exhibition Society (1888) heralded the Arts and Craft Movement. Its aim was to revive handicrafts and reunite them into building design. Painted friezes, stained glass, woodcarvings began to once again adorn buildings. Further integration of art continued into the early 1900s. Architects began to include murals, mosaics, sculptures and other works of art into large public and commercial buildings. However towards the end of the 19th century engineers were demanding more accuracy and axonometric projections and three dimensional geometric represent-ations were considered by some to be more objective forms of communication. The beginning of the 20th century heralded a distinct change in architectural representation. Drawings were based less on visual intuition, and a more academic approach was adopted for their production. The period of the Modern Movement signalled a time of increasing industrial technology and saw a revival in the use of physical scale models to represent buildings. Drawings became symbolic rather than literal, with architects expressing their design intention without decoration, although the technique of perspective was still applied. Indeed *throughout the 19th century and up to the advent of CAD the perspective drawing remained the traditional way for an architect to demonstrate to his employer, what the results of his investment would be. It sought to provide a realistic impression of the intended finished product* (Fellows 1998).

The skill and artistic licence of the architect in presenting his ideas have led to questions concerning the relationship between drawing and building. In considering the work of Edwin Alfred Rickards, a partner of Lanchester, Stewart and Rickards, Fellows (1998) notes *he was able to produce marvellously fluent drawings, particularly of detail and ornament, which, one feels, could have been translated from the paper into reality. The immediacy of the inspiration is conveyed in the building . . .* It may be claimed that there is an interactive relationship between the drawing and the product that it is aiming to illustrate. At a base level, it is probable the building and its drawing have a common style. However the relationship can be much deeper. The architect may be even subconsciously trying to visualize the very ethos of the design philosophy, through the drawing. For the artist–architect, this is a natural association and the drawing can become part of the design process (Fellows 1998).

There have been many times, however, when architects did not produce their own representations, but employed independent artists. The Picturesque Movement at the end of the 18th century saw architects beginning to employ professional watercolour artists to illustrate their ideas. Many qualified architects acknowledged that their real love was in the representation of architecture, whether via drawing, painting, sketching, model making or digital art. Some worked alongside practising architects, but chose to focus on the visualization of design ideas. Naturally some important and longstanding relationships developed between artists and architects – *The production of art, as much as any other production, takes place in the context of human interaction – with others, with nature, with tools, with artifacts, and with ideas from times passed* (Nadin 1989). Artists required skill, patience and trust to successfully envisage the idea in the mind of an architect. The introduction of architectural competitions in the 19th century resulted in further employment of professional independent artists to produce presentations of the highest quality. Societies were formed which acknowledged the importance of these independent artists, model makers and computer illustrators, and their contribution as professionals and craftsmen in the field of architecture became well recognized. At the end of the 20th century the traditional lines of distinction between advertising, public relations, architecture, computer programming, and graphic design were blurring (Buday 2000). *Again, we are at a point where paradigms are shifting, synthesis is occurring, balances of power are being unbalanced, worlds are being hyperlinked and professional boundaries are disappearing* (Spiller 2000). Architectural practice was becoming *multi-discipline* and larger practices either employed their own artists to work on a variety of media, or they commissioned work from those independent artists who had formed their own companies. Successful independent artists have always had to keep abreast with developments of their time, applying new tools and techniques to architectural representation. Yet the aim of the independent artist can be different to that of the architect. Whereas the architect's aim in a visualization is to communicate ideas, an artist is concerned with generating meaning, with revealing the nature of their medium and their relationship to it (Wright 1989). Fellows (1998), developing his claim about the association between drawing and design process, is concerned that where either the personnel or the means are more detached, there may be more apprehension as to whether the drawing is a faithful representation of the future building. In particular as architects' offices were becoming increasingly computerized, and the need for drawing skills was becoming less important, the CAD software that was used could well have an effect on built work.

Concern and debate on the validity of images that represent architecture has had a long history, with conflicting attitudes to the art of drawing, the eye-catching perspectives of the 19th century, and the computer-generated representations of the 20th century. Issues of *skill*, *honesty*, and *artistic licence* apply to all forms of architectural representation and should be considered in any analysis of correlation between architectural representation and eventual building (Stamp 1982).

If an architectural representation is to be effective in demonstrating to a client what the results of his investment will be, the process of its production needs to be reliable, and the final image credible, if it is to carry any measure of authority. The creation of a realistic impression where the object does not exist, is a particular skill (Stamp 1982). *Skills* required for effective architectural representation have gathered over many hundreds of years and architects have accumulated an impressive portfolio of expertise, developed alongside educational advancements and technical innovations. Although tools and media may change in function and form, and some are long forgotten, many of the skills of the architect are as important today as they ever were. Architects have long analysed existing structures by sketching, then incorporated ideas from these sketches into new designs. Broadbent (1989) describes this approach as *You like this building, so you are going to record it as seductively as you can, making the sketch itself into a beautiful thing: the medium itself takes over, conditioning what it is you sketch.* Sketching, whether for recording details of an existing building, or for forming ideas for a new building, has remained an essential skill of the architect. An understanding of drawing, painting, colour, three dimensional geometric representations, isometric perspective and sciagraphy is still required to create and communicate the essence of design. Whether using blank paper, empty canvas, modelling clay, or computer screen, certain fundamentals still apply, and possession of knowledge and skill in these areas can only result in a more credible representation. The growing ease with which it is possible to select options from a computer menu, to perform tasks that used to be in the domain of craftsmen, does not lessen the need for an artistic eye, together with an understanding of the craft the machine is performing.

Prior to the establishment of formal architectural education, architects learnt their trade by observation of the work of influential architects or respected theorists, past or present. Publications of creditable doctrine were translated into various languages and eventually published in the form of practical manuals, disseminating principles to those in practice. The development of new drawing aids and instruments, drawing and graphic techniques, as well as many realized and unrealized designs were all recorded in a variety of published works. Collections of drawings also provided a valuable resource for students of architecture seeking to adopt the style of inspirational architects. Those students fortunate enough to be employed in architectural practice learnt from their employers, some of whom were good teachers, keen to inspire and encourage. Pupils could help in the production of architectural publications, and although they received no formal architectural education, their powers of observation, and other skills developed in apprenticeship, were valuable for the future. Those with the means to do so would travel to places of architectural significance to study both building design and conserved drawings. The formation of influential societies, guilds and academies over the years improved and added to the range of skills of the architect, as well as providing respected forums for the exhibition of proposed architectural designs, competition entries and topographical depictions.

The development of full-time architectural education did not begin in England until the beginning of the 20th century. Architectural courses became recognized at universities, following the approach set at Liverpool University, under C H Reilly. The system of articled pupillage of previous years, where students learnt their craft from their masters, was to be replaced by a scheme modelled on the French Beaux Arts system, and versions practised in the United States. The systematic preparation of a Beaux Arts drawing is recalled by Broadbent (1989): *You stretched a sheet of paper, drew your Renaissance composition in meticulous detail, cast the shadows and then rendered it with up to 40 washes of hand-ground, and filtered, sepia ink.*

At the beginning of the 21st century the digital revolution was accompanied with concern for the integration of digital methods into architectural design and presentation. The introduction of computers to students of architecture was influenced by factors such as available resources, enthusiasm of staff, pressure from students, direction from professional bodies and prejudices in favour of the more traditional techniques. Nonetheless students of many schools of architecture at the beginning of the 21st century were demonstrating that skill in design and traditional drawing could be combined with the new skills of computer modelling, rendering and animation (Clary 2000). Indeed architectural practice was looking to employ young graduates who had an aptitude for the new technology, so they could further its integration into practice. In a discussion of *cyberspace*, a term used by William Mitchell, Pickering (1996) predicts that the architect's skill in transforming *artistic impulse into material expression* could be of enormous benefit to the forces that are bringing cyberspace into being.

As well as the skill of the architect, or artist, in visual communication, credibility of an image could be improved by evidence of *preciseness* and *honesty* in the process of its production. The accuracy of architectural representations has long been a subject of reflection and debate. Architects have had a wide range of drawing aids with which to work over the years, and Harris (1982) claims that there is no doubt that the constant high quality of architectural drawings throughout the centuries is due to the high precision of drawing instruments. From the early 18th century many established north European architects published their works to attract further patronage. The tradition of publication demanded clear and accurate representation, and mathematical drawing instruments were used to meet these demands (Hambly 1982). Accuracy was certainly required for the correct representation of the classical orders. Specialist pens were developed to aid geometrical drawing. Broadbent (1989) comments that axonometric drawings of architects such as Stirling, Eisenman and Krier would not have been possible before the development of the Rapidograph pen (1952) and Rotring's Isograph pen (1977). The introduction of the rationalized steel frame from America (early 1990s) contributed to black and white, precise engineering-like drawings with figured dimensions which could be reproduced easily. CAD images, based on mathematical processes, are supposed to be precise, and the computer can indeed perform calculations to impressive degrees of accuracy. The initial data which form the basis of the model need to be derived from accurate sources. Functions are built into software to support and encourage accuracy in modelling and to eliminate guesswork. For visualizations that began life in 2D format, then extruded into 3D, accuracy was vital as the subsequent rendering process could highlight any flaws in initial geometry.

Issues of *honesty* are also of as much concern today as they have been in the past. The following chapters touch on the honesty of the architect, and the recognition by some architects that their preferred mode of presentation had limitations. There has been mistrust recorded about many types of presentation, and the level of detail incorporated. The current trend of clients becoming involved *earlier* in the design process has led to a belief by some computer illustrators that simpler renderings are preferable to those with artistic finishes. A presentation may gain influence by being full of detail, but it may also lead to clients' reluctance to suggest changes. There is an honesty in rendering a building from an accurately constructed computer model. Simple renderings can still possess an artistic elegance and clients can be very enthusiastic about the opportunity to view a design as a quickly rendered computer model (Claridge 1996). Therefore simple, accurate representation, presented honestly to the client to help explore design possibilities has its place in today's world, where even the most complex buildings are expected in less time and at less cost.

In addition to the skill and honesty of the architect or artist and the precision of the tools and media, the issue of *artistic licence* is a consideration in any study on architectural representation. In examining the role of the traditional perspective Gavin Stamp (1982) says, *the perspective is not an essential part of the architect's job, nor is it a precise tool in the difficult process of turning a design into a building. Rather it belongs to both art and architecture. It is an ARTIST'S IMPRESSION and the success of a perspective depends on artistic imagination and skill. So, while building designs are approved by clients without a perspective view of what the building will look like, nevertheless it can provide a bridge between the architect and an often-uncomprehending public. As such, it is as useful today as ever.* However some believed that the nature of a drawing could obscure the reality of a building (Stamp 1982). It is possible that the self-expression of the artist, his *artistic licence*, may not always provide a clear picture of what a building might be like. Fellows (1998), in discussing the trend, in the early 1990s, of architects to employ professional perspectivists points out that *the draughtsmen all worked to their own particular styles, which on some occasions were not really appropriate for the subject matter and emphasized fashionable approaches and techniques.* In today's busy practices there is some belief that computer representations are getting close to work produced by professional artists; *you can do walk-through perspectives with solid and transparent planes, coloured and shaded, with highlights and reflections. Even better when by skilful use of video you can put real people in, moving around, changing scale in perspective as they do so. And once you've added sound, smell, temperature . . .* (Broadbent 1989). Skilled use of today's technology is aiming to provide an '*almost real*' experience, rather than simply an *impression,* of a building. Yet in the quest to provide a new realism, there remain concerns that fashionable technology can be used indiscriminately. Doubts are raised as to whether this new media, impressive for its accuracy and preciseness, could ever lend itself to *art*. Wright (1989) stated that computer imagery can give the impression of having a greater clarity than an ordinary photograph, as each object projects itself on our retina as forcibly as the next . . . *it is difficult to resist the feeling that the artist has tried to insist upon the superior reality of the computed image by giving all the elements in the scene an equal, idealized definition, that is how things really look without the limitations of the human eye.* Some believed that such visualizations were not providing the sort of realism that lends credibility and authority to an artist's impression: *as opposed to works of art that look better the more we look at them, electronic art seems to exhaust itself at the first encounter. There are numerous instances in which the computer controls the artist and 'signs' the work* (Nadin 1989). There is a need for the technology to *disappear*, to become *invisible*. This criticism of computer art, and concern with *realism*, is understandable. Reaction to new forms of art, and architecture, is rarely without conflict.

Aristotle, considered to be the originator of realism, believed that works of art should not be literal copies of nature but should express the *essence* of the subject portrayed (Jones 1989). Two schools of thought have developed on the subject of representation, and are described by Coyne (1994) as the *constructivist* view and the *correspondence* view. The constructivist school of thought argues that representation is a cultural phenomenon and that the quality and appropriateness of a representation depends on its purpose. The correspondence view argues that a representation corresponds to what is out there in the object: *if we can capture the basic geometry of the world in a computer system, then the representation of this information is an accurate reconstruction of reality.* Architects select those properties of a building considered necessary to preserve in a representation. The selection will depend on the purpose of the representation, but for architecture, geometrical description is usually considered fundamental. Beyond that, how much detail is required and where emphasis should be placed are but two of the questions only answered by clearly identifying the purpose of the work, and thereafter establishing whether a subjective or objective representation is appropriate. *Photo-realism* may not be always what is required.

As new tools and techniques became fashionable for architectural representation, a preoccupation with these often resulted in a diversion to the matter in hand, the representation of a building. Claridge (1996) remarked that *in traditional media, artists are often recognizable in their work. With computer rendering, it is sometimes easier to recognize the software than the artist behind it. The challenge seems to be in finding efficiency in the tools without allowing them to compromise or pre-empt the design intent.*

The prescriptiveness of computer systems had been a major preoccupation of researchers during the 1980s and 1990s, with concern that standard elements included in the software package were being built in real life. Practices were finding it easier to select a less-than-ideal object from a ready-to-render symbol library than to create an ideal one from scratch (Claridge 1996). Some questioned whether this prescriptiveness encouraged designers to modify their design proposals to fit the constraints imposed by a system, and if so, whether this had any effect on architecture (Tweed 1999). There was also concern that the conventions embedded in the hardware, software and imagery of computer graphics could limit the models that may be generated (Jones 1989). Architects and artists have always been presented with new tools and media for design and presentation, but it was the pre-configured nature of the computer, full of defaults and short-cuts, that gave cause for concern to the profession at the end of the 20th century.

So what of the *correlation between architectural representation and eventual building*? Many of the elements which influence architecture – social forces, technology, orientation, movement, context and ecology (Crosbie 2000) also influence visual art, and therefore it may be reasonable to contemplate that there is a connection between the style of a building and the way it is represented. The examples that follow in *Artists' Impressions* offer some contemplation on this hypothesis. Lee Dunnette is an architectural illustrator who has worked with world famous architects for many years. He reflected, in correspondence, that *it is important to make a distinction between impressions produced during the design process, and impressions presented to the client at a later stage, when the design is more defined. There is evidence to show that the visualizing techniques of architects, whether drawings, paintings, physical models or computer simulations, used during the design process, are directly related to the final design of the building. However the presentation techniques of architects, when showing their design to the client, are related to the design visualizing techniques, but may not be the same.* The process of conveying an idea from the mind of the architect to the medium of exploration, to the medium of explanation, then to the completed building, is rarely accomplished without some deviation.

With so much current speculation and debate about the impact of information technology on current architectural practice it is only by glimpsing into history that we can put some perspective on the rapidly evolving techniques of today. The use of computers in architecture is still at an early stage. However architecture is no stranger to scientific innovation and change, much of which has had some influence on representation and built form. The following chapters explore the variety of ways prospective buildings have been represented, and offer a reflection on *artists' impressions in architectural design*.

2.0   Perspective Drawing
Sebastiano Serlio 1611

Chapter 2 Theory and Ideas about Envisioning Buildings

2.1   **Witley Court, Great Witley, Worcestershire**
J Wood 1843

Great architects were not necessarily great draughtsmen. For example, while Inigo Jones was considered to be one of the finest draughtsmen in Europe, there is much more debate about the quality of Christopher Wren's drawings (Lever and Richardson 1983, Summerson 1966). The situation becomes even less clear where architects of renown established substantial offices in which other architects and pupils were employed. In such circumstances it is often difficult to tell who was actually responsible for the drawings and in some cases the designs as well. In England, standards of drafting were to improve following the foundation of the Royal Academy of Arts in 1768. When at the end of the 18th century, picturesque architecture came into fashion in the work of architects like **John Nash** (1752–1835) it became almost obligatory to compose designs as pictures. As well as line and wash, presentations were required in watercolour paintings. As a result, professional watercolour artists were increasingly engaged by architects to illustrate their designs in flamboyant style. Many of the illustrators were architects themselves, and it is interesting to speculate on how much they were responsible for developing the designs as

they drew them.By the early years of the 19th century, it had become almost impossible in many cases to distinguish between a topographical view and an architectural design. This depiction of Whitley Court is a topographical view by Wood, although it could almost equally well be one of Repton's c. 1810 design drawings for Nash. From the turn of the century, perspectivists were much in demand especially in the larger architectural offices. The Royal Academy Exhibition had become an important venue for attracting commissions and perspective artists produced many of the exhibits which seemed to increase in size as the 19th century progressed (Lever and Richardson 1983). According to Blomfield (1912), there are clear differences in architectural drawings related to their purpose. The intention for creating them may be either objective or subjective, i.e. generated to produce a building exactly as drawn or to allow an impression of the building to be formed in someone else's mind. Farey and Edwards (1931) point out that as owners are spending considerable sums on these projects, they should be able to demand a realistic impression of the building as well as the kind of factual information for construction. It sounds so

simple – the architect just needs to offer *a realistic impression of the building* but this statement is at the heart of the discussion. Even Goodhart-Rendel's (1951) proclamation that the perspective drawing *is the dishonest architect's most artful and convenient confederate* does not really explain the various forces at work. As Gavin Stamp (1982) says, it is actually to do with skill as well as honesty and the notion of artistic licence undermines some of the assurance about a correlation between the eventual building and its representation. Spiers (1887) notes that a perspective can never *convey the ultimate effect of the building because it is limited to one fixed point of view.* Presumably, therefore, he was advocating models as the only means of securing unlimited views of the proposals. Adams (1901) adds more doubt about the effectiveness of pictorial representation in his conclusion that *the more we realize that perspectives are at best architectural diagrams, the better for good building.* Perspective drawing was not used in early art forms. It does not occur in ancient Egyptian or Greek art. The geometric theory and practical system for these drawings were actually developed during the Renaissance (Diekman and Pile 1983).

In the 15th century, architecture came to be understood as a liberal art and architectural ideas were increasingly conceived as geometric two dimensional drawings. Filippo Brunelleschi (1377–1446) is credited with the earliest example of a systematically constructed linear perspective in 1420. On a small, rectangular wooden panel, Brunelleschi painted a symmetrical representation of the octagonal baptistery in Florence's Piazza San Giovanni. He then perforated the panel at the vanishing point and asked observers to verify the correctness of the representation by looking through the orifice from the back of the panel toward a mirror that the observer held in the other hand. In Renaissance treatises on perspective drawing, binocular vision was often reduced to a single point of view. One of the most influential pioneers was **Sebastiano Serlio** (1475–1554) whose book has arguably even eclipsed *De Pictura (1485)* by the great Leon Battista Alberti (1401–1472) as a model for subsequent treatises. According to Serlio, no perspectivist could do his work without architecture nor could there be architecture without perspective. Possibly this was an evangelical view by someone at the forefront of perspective development surrounded by the ubiquitous *lineamenti*. He based his initial one point perspective technique on the triangle and used it to set out a number of geometric figures. Examples are the hexagon and the circle, in which the plan was the generator. He discovered that this system could be used for any plan where projected or real features cross the diagonal. It works well for two dimensional figures like plans but Serlio needed to develop it for three dimensional elements such as columns. One significant difference is that the column appears essentially in elevation and without depth, unless the observer is positioned to the side.

2.2

2.3

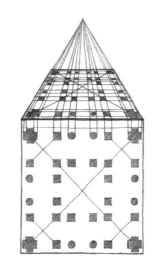

2.4

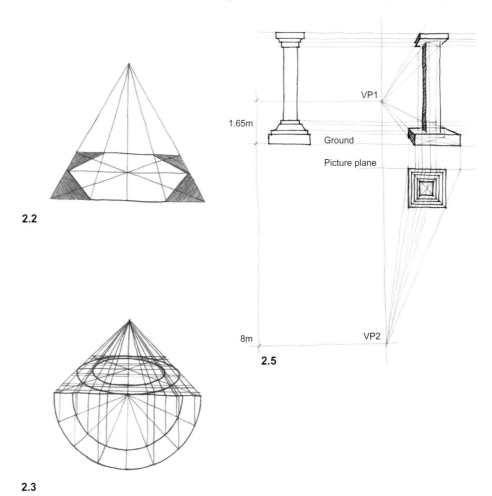

2.5

The height of the observer as shown by vanishing point VP1, becomes quite significant as the human scale can imply the size of an element and determine whether it is seen from above or below. In this way, architectural composition can be viewed in one point perspective. While the scale of the plan can be used to determine the height and eye level of the observer, Serlio (1611) is rather vague about how the depth is obtained. It can be achieved by trial and error but as a theory, which can be tested and replicated precisely, it is not easy to follow without a more precise geometry – the perspectives can become distorted.

The most recent textbooks on architectural drawing state that the one point perspective is more suitable for interior views or the surroundings of buildings which are themselves shown in elevation. In this case, the scale of the plan relates to the back wall of the space or the building elevation, and the eye-level of the observer scaled accordingly. The position and distance of the observer need to be chosen and can be scaled if required. The depth is determined within a 90° field of vision that generates two vanishing points (VP2 and VP3) to either side. Projection from the observer through positions on the plan to the picture plane and then vertically to the ground line – intersecting lines from VP2 or VP3 – provide intermediate depths (McCarthy 1996). It is interesting to apply this approach to Serlio's models. The adjacent drawing shows the hexagon reproduced in single point perspective by using the 20th century technique of three vanishing points. In all perspective drawing, the construction lines should be very light but clearly and accurately drawn. The slightest error can easily become greatly exaggerated and distort the whole drawing. It is a useful technique but has distinct limitations. For symmetrical shapes it is fine but cannot cope with asymmetry.

Serlio (1611) muses that *as I thought to make an end of my second book, I begin to handle a harder matter . . . it is as well drawn by the horizon as by the distances, as you may see in the figure following.* He had begun to consider the two point perspective. Serlio goes on to develop this principle with a number of geometric figures but when it comes to the architectural and natural perspective scenes at the end of the second book, they are all in one point perspective (see Fig. 2.0) indicating that the two point variety had not reached a position in which it could be freely used.

2.6

2.7

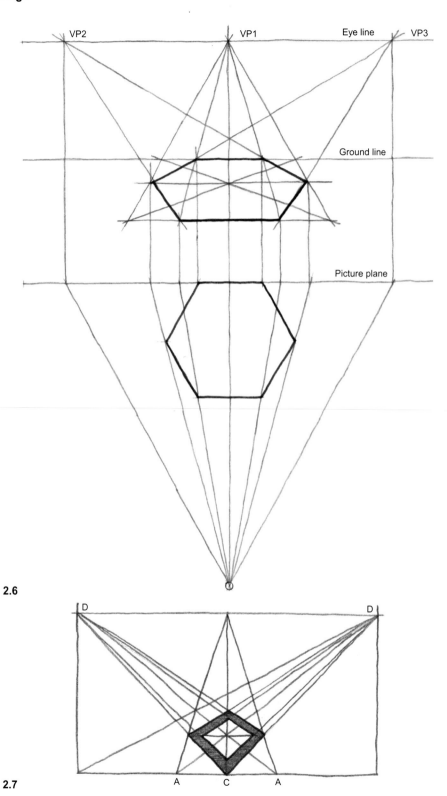

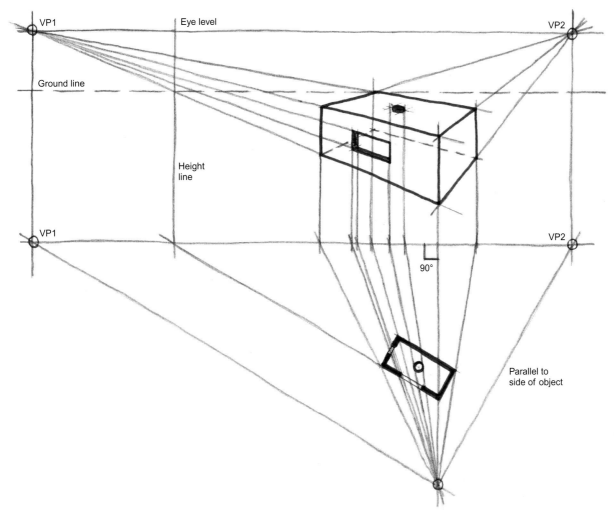

VP1   Eye level   VP2

Ground line

Height
line

VP1   VP2

90°

Parallel to
side of object

2.8

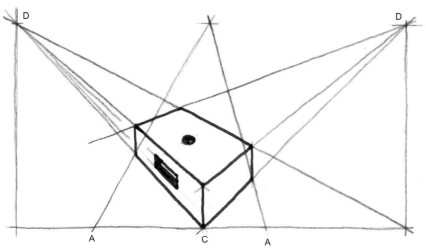

D   D

A   C   A

2.9

By the latter part of the 20th century, the above had become the generally accepted method of constructing two point perspectives. The observer does not have to look directly at the corner of the object but it does simplify the method to do so. It is recommended that the line of vision should not bisect the object or the effect will be spoiled. Serlio's symmetrical approach is starting to look too limited for general application. A good way of positioning an asymetrical line of vision could be to draw lines from the observer to the limits of the building (McCarthy 1996).

Alternatively, it has been discovered from experimentation that the angle of vision between these lines should be between 40° and 60°, and bisected to find the line of vision. The picture plane must always be at right angles to the line of vision and the angle between the lines, drawn to locate the vanishing points, must also be a right angle. This method seems to favour rectilinear shapes. Other geometric or irregular shapes need to be enclosed in a framework of straight lines. Geometrical perspectives have been criticized for their mechanistic appearance, although in machine-age architecture this would probably have been an advantage. At the opposite end of the spectrum, the picturesque philosophy relies totally on the artist's eye, which led to the accusations of inaccuracy and even deceit. A common form of illustration depicts the building in two dimensions whereas the foreground is in perspective. Depending on one's attitude, this can be perceived as a rapid and attractive way of showing the building in context or the use of depth of foreground with trees and foliage to conveniently obscure some unfortunate aspect of the design.

The convention in drawing that shows three dimensional objects in two dimensions is known as orthogonal or orthographic projection. This is a popular form of illustration but demands a leap of imagination to consider how a building might appear in the round. The views are generally plan, elevations and sections where:

- *A plan can be a view vertically downwards on top of a building but more usually is a horizontal slice through a building taken at a position that gives most information, often through the windows just above sill height.*

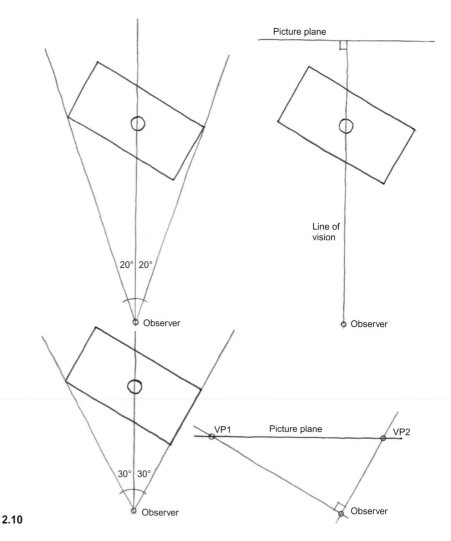

2.10

- *Elevations show the vertical planes derived from the plan, retaining their true size, shape and detail.*
- *A section is a cross-cut made vertically through the building. It should show the interior of the far wall in elevation.*

One of the fundamentals in architectural representation is the creation of depth in a two dimensional medium. Depth takes on greater significance than just another dimension. The height and width are real but the depth is in a way, an illusion conceived by the architect or artist through drawing technique. Arguably, the more

honest approach could be to merely show planar surfaces in two dimensions and allow the observer to put them together as an impression of a three dimensional building. Views should be to the same scale and are often aligned with one another. Material which is actually cut through in plan or section is shown in a much stronger manner than information in elevation or on the floor of the plan. Engineering drawings are arranged differently according to whether they are in first or third angle projection but the arrangement in architecture is generally as follows.

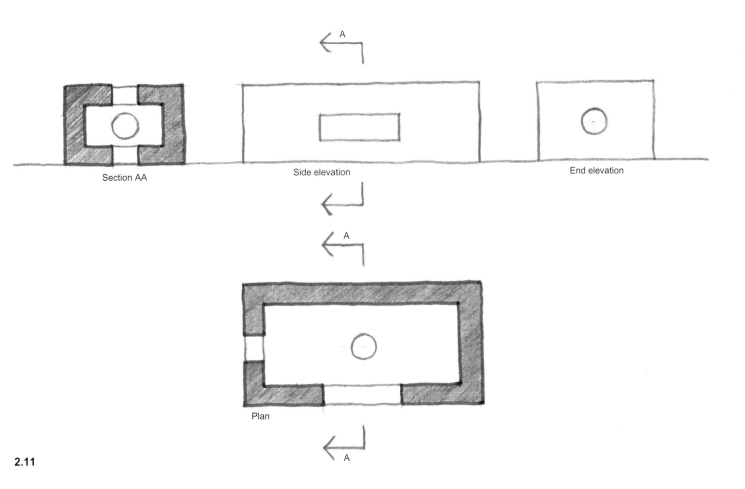

Section AA   Side elevation   End elevation

Plan

2.11

In the early years of the 20th century, academics such as CH Reilly (1874–1948) became increasingly attracted by American practice and in 1909 he spent several months in the United States to study the new breed of architects. It increased his enthusiasm for the grand manner of McKim (1849–1909), Mead (1856–1906) and White (1848–1928), and Daniel H Burnham (1846–1912) of Chicago. Drawings were based on the French Beaux Arts system with its emphasis on plans, sections and elevations. Sometimes they look like abstract patterns in their own right and the drawings almost became an end in themselves. Reilly introduced this system into the Liverpool University School of Architecture and it swept into the new full-time architectural courses throughout the country. Very rapidly, the free and easy nature of Edwardian Baroque, which was based on visual judgement associated with picture-making, was replaced by drawings of monumental designs in a restrained and academic manner (Fellows 1998). However, as early as the 19th century, there had been those who wished to present three dimensional geometric impressions. Axonometric, isometric and oblique projections were seen as ways of combining the accuracy of plan and elevation with the overall effect of perspective. If plans are seen as either looking downwards onto the top of a building or as a horizontal slice through it, axonometric projection contains true plans. The principal angle is 45° and the vertical lines are also true to scale. As drawing instruments developed into drafting machines, geometric accuracy became a particularly useful property in readily showing bird's eye and worm's eye views. The new instruments also contributed to changes in the building designs. Idiosyncratic expression appeared less as rectilinear forms tended to take over.

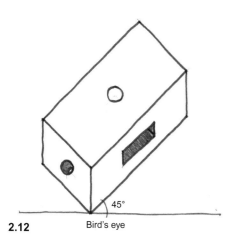

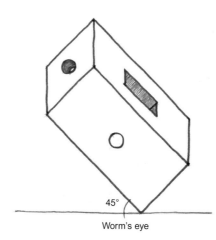

2.12   Bird's eye   Worm's eye

Historically there was a notion that isometrics were *deceptive* perspectives but generally it has been accepted that they are perspectives constructed with vanishing points postulated at infinity. The outcome is that lines which are in reality parallel, remain parallel in the drawing. The importance was celebrated by William Farrish in *Isometrical Perspective* (1820) and by Joseph Jopling in *The Practice of Isometrical Perspective* (1835). Farrish points out that *it represents straight lines, which lie in three principal directions, all on the same scale.*

Axonometric projection was taught in Engineering Schools from the late 19th century, for its usefulness as an accurate technical tool. In the architectural world, Augustus Choisy was the first author to use axonometric projections extensively. In his famous works on the history of architecture, published between 1873 and 1899, he used mostly worm's eye views. Choisy claimed that orthogonal projections were abstractions that fragmented the representation into plan, section and elevation. Whereas, the axonometric was one image showing an integrated view of the plan, exterior, section and interior disposition – accurately accompanied by scale. At the 1923 De Stijl exhibition, axonometric drawing was presented as a privileged vehicle for conceiving the architecture of space. Yet, for many people, this kind of projection seems to distort both form and space as the back corner appears too pronounced. Writers on modern architecture have often emphasized the polarity between perspectives and axonometrics. The latter is seen as an objective tool whereas the former is perceived as an illusionist representation of a building in its context. Also, the axonometric has invariably been regarded as a drawing by architects for architects,

while the perspective has been the means of presenting a project to the client. However, this is not exclusively the case. Even in the 19th century, some architects became suspicious of perspectives, believing them to be deceptive painting techniques. Axonometrics extended previous ideas of three dimensional representation, a step further into precise objectivity. It was a totally novel concept as well as a more powerful means of control and co-ordination. It became the expression of the paradigm of high modernity, portraying the same mentality and assumptions that would eventually allow for architectural design through computer graphics (Perez-Gomez and Pelletier 1997). The terms used to describe parallel projections in European languages have changed from time to time and this has caused some confusion. Axonometrics have been defined as special cases of isometrics and vice versa. Yet there are major theoretical differences. As already demonstrated, the first technique has been universally seen as the antithesis of the perspective whereas the second can be considered as a form of perspective. This may seem like playing with semantics but the two have never really appeared as equivalent alternatives to each other.

It is important to remember that isometrics do not preserve any *real* angles. Consequently, a kind of distortion is also apparent in this form of projection as it does not demonstrate a true plan or elevation. In the mid 20th century, there were attempts to reduce the apparent distortion by introducing an isometric scale. Nevertheless, this turned out to be an additional complication with the disadvantage of changing some of the dimensions so that they were no longer true scale and it was soon dropped while the technique enjoyed a late 20th century revival.

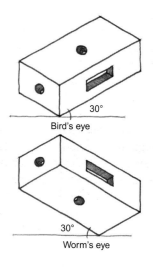

2.13

Bird's eye

Worm's eye

There are two variations of oblique projection. In the first, the oblique lines are drawn at 45° to the front elevation. In the second, the oblique lines are drawn at 30°. The same scale is used for horizontal and vertical lines and half scale for the oblique line in the 45° version, and the same scale throughout for the 30° model. The difference is interesting and relates to previous observations about the nature of drawing depth. The first of these two variations has a perspective quality about it, while the second appears to be a little twisted and the depth elongated.

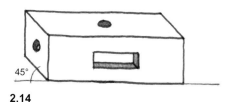 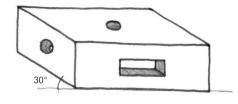

2.14

Gavin Stamp (1982) makes the point that the geometrical representation offered by orthographic and three dimensional projections ought to be able to convey precise information for planning committees, building control officers, constructors and so on; but to the untutored layman they convey rather less about the intended appearance of the building. He claims that such geometrical drawings are abstractions as they represent the design in the form of stylized depictions rather than as the building would be viewed in reality. On the other hand, in his treatise on perspective, Daniele Barbaro (1569) devotes an entire section to perspective illusion. He seems to be saying that while perspective is important in art, architecture requires a precision that should be provided by plan and elevation. He concludes that perspective alters dimensions and therefore cannot be relied upon. This debate only started in the Renaissance because previously architectural drawings were rare and arguments about the style and appearance of a building took place while it was being constructed. The debate about drawing style took on an increasing significance as impressions of the proposals became essential before the work could begin.

Alberti also made much of the difference between the drawings of a painter and those of an architect. In *De Re Aedificatoria (1485)*, he notes that while a painter *takes pains to emphasize the relief of objects in paintings with shading and diminishing lines*, the architect draws as if his work would be judged *not by the apparent perspective* nor *by deceptive appearances* but *exactly on the basis of controllable measures*. He insisted that simple models should be used to bridge the gap between the geometric *lineamenti* and the volume of the building. Bertotti Scamozzi (1719–1790) claimed that the word *scenographia* in Vitruvius meant *model* as opposed to *painting* or *delineation*. He goes on to define two kinds of perspective, one of which he says is no use to architects. The Renaissance *artificial* perspective, as theorised by Serlio, must be abandoned in favour of the *natural* perspective. Seemingly the point here is that the former contains optical distortions that can be rectified by the latter. According to John Ruskin (1819–1900), all great architects of the past had been great painters or sculptors as well. On this basis, he relentlessly chided Victorian architects to study painting and sculpture if they ever hoped to achieve anything. His love of universal talents which

seemed so abundant in the architects of previous centuries, strengthened his contempt for the professional demarcations of the time. It also fed his rather eccentric theory that building only became architecture when painting and sculpture were added to grace a structurally adequate skeleton (Saint 1983). The system for selecting designs on a competitive basis, particularly for important public buildings, is a recurring theme in *Artists' Impressions*. It became extremely popular in the 19th century and still holds a strong position in world architecture today. Nevertheless, it has had a chequered history and unless carefully controlled, architectural competitions are readily open to abuse. The position became so unsavoury in Victorian times that many established practices and some eminent architects refused to take part in them. A major criticism was that they were invariably assessed by laymen who could, as the competitions committee of the Institute of Architects reported in 1839, *select a design without suspecting in the slightest degree that they may have been captivated by the meretricious allurements of the artist*. Alternatively, it could be argued that competition drawings should provide images of ideas rather than blueprints for construction.

Towards the end of the 19th century, architects became increasingly torn between a romantic dream and the realities of a commercial society. Superb and highly idealized watercolour perspectives frequently possessed greater aesthetic merit than the proposed buildings that they represented. Their authors were severely criticized to the point of accusations about flagrant dishonesty. Yet, it seems likely that most of these drawings were not so much dishonest attempts to win the confidence of unwitting clients and more the yearnings of romantic artists, frustrated by the environment in which they found themselves. Sadly, the dreams of the romantic artists were transitory. Pugin's *New Jerusalem* could not be reconciled with Victorian material progress (Jenkins 1963). As modernism beckoned, the moral handle was that perspectives were misleading. As such, they might fool clients and therefore should not be used to depict buildings. However, the lack of them started to fool the architects themselves as they began to lose the ability to visualize the three dimensional forms of their intended buildings (Cullinan 1998).

3.0 **Façade Project for a Venetian Palace**
Andrea Palladio c. 1554

Early practice in predicting the final appearance of buildings included full-size drawings which were produced anywhere from the tracing lofts of craftsmen to the floors of noblemen's palaces. In fact, right up to the mid 20th century, realization was in the hands of builders and craftsmen working to *design* drawings. The main representation was through sketches with formal drawings indicating only the broad nature of the construction. It was the creative skills that were celebrated. The presentation of his centralized church designs by **Leonardo da Vinci** (1452–1519) used solid exterior views in perspective, plan and sometimes sections. It is closely related to the system of demonstration used in his skull studies at that time. This drawing is one of a series of intricate variations on a centralized theme which seem to have been stimulated by his work on a project for Milan Cathedral. He devoted much time and thought to the study of perspective. Cellini even spoke of seeing a manuscript by Leonardo, containing *the most beautiful discourse on perspective ever composed* but this seems to have been lost (Kemp *et al.* 1989).

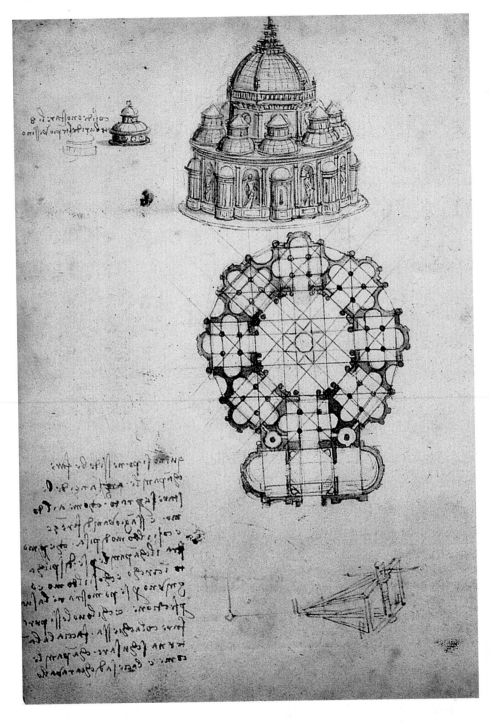

3.1 Design for Centralized Temple
Leonardo da Vinci c. 1488

In Medieval England, the eventual buildings were often the result of several contributions – for example, the original rough plan may have been by one man, possibly the owner for whom it was being built. This would require interpretation and details to be added (Summerson 1991). The most important secondary contribution would be an impression of what the building might look like. Thus there is some difficulty in determining responsibility for much medieval architecture (Kaye 1960) especially as skilled masons and carpenters invariably provided the details and sometimes the principal elevations for stone and timber constructions to be erected by themselves and others. They worked in teams of craftsmen in quite a hierarchical manner, each headed by a master. In these days of pre-industrialization, the cathedrals, churches and great houses on which they worked were geographically spread out. So the teams would tour the country in search of their next project. Perhaps not surprisingly, very few of the drawings actually survived. So the obscurity in which the Smythsons worked is not particular to them. In fact, the **Smythson** archive at the Royal Institute of British Architects Drawings Collection reveals as much about them as any of their contemporaries. **Robert** (1535–1614) and his son **John** (c. 1570–1634) were primarily masons who developed the ability to plan out their ideas on paper and parchment, in a carefully conceived way before starting to undertake the construction work. The close relationship which they clearly enjoyed with their aristocratic clients must have included presentation of the drawings for discussion and approval. The design of the bay at Longleat is a remarkably precise drawing for its time. According to Girouard (1966), it is also probably the earliest surviving drawing by Robert Smythson. As one house develops from another, there was an original mind and strong imagination at work. Thus, the proposition that Robert was one of the creators of the Elizabethan Style is not far fetched (Girouard 1966). As a drawing, John's design for a room in the Little Castle at Bolsover Castle may appear rather quirky, especially with the cut-out flaps for window shutters (see Fig 3.4). However, as Lever and Richardson (1983) point out, its real interest lies in the fact that it is the earliest English example of an interior perspective in the RIBA Collection.

3.2   Design for a Bay at Longleat, Wiltshire
Robert Smythson c. 1568

3.3   Design for a Country House
Robert Smythson 1590

Jacques Gentilhâtre (1578–c. 1623) is described as an architect but like the Smythsons he, too, was probably a master mason. He seems to have been connected with the du Cerceau atelier, a notable family architectural practice. Apparently, he spent most of his formative years with them, and throughout his life the architecture of the de Cerceau atelier is evident in his own drawings. It has been suggested that as all the principals of that practice died within a relatively short period, he inherited their architectural ideas. Except for a few of his most elaborate buildings, Gentilhâtre never deviated from this decorative drawing style, which was becoming increasingly out of fashion. Compared with de Brosse and Mansart, he appeared firmly rooted in the past (Coope 1972). Little information is available, especially about the latter part of his life, and it is only possible to speculate whether he was unable to move on or whether the influence of the de Cerceaux was so strong within him or whether he was really a mason who could copy but not create. Nevertheless, his drawings provide a valuable record of a period that has largely been lost.

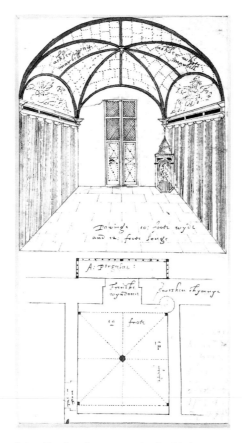

3.4   Design for a room in the Little Castle, Bolsover Castle, Derbyshire
John Smythson 1625

3.5   Design for a pavilion at Charleval
Jacques Gentilhâtre c. 1600

Andrea Palladio (1508–1589) has been the most imitated architect in history, and his influence on the development of English and American architecture is probably greater than that of all other Renaissance architects combined. To many generations his designs seemed to be the perfect embodiment of the classical tradition. The most significant aspect in his work is the relationship of the parts to the whole (Ackerman 1966). In 1570, he produced *I Quattro Libri dell' Architettura* while working in Venice. The four books form a treatise on the *fundamentals of architecture and the orders, domestic design* (mainly his own) *public and urban design and engineering*, and *temples*. English translations followed in the early 18th century, along with the first versions of pattern books. Authors such as William Halfpenny (c. 1723–1775) and Batty Langley (1696–1751) published these practical manuals which made sense of high architectural aims for the benefit of craftsmen and their patrons (Tavernor 1991). Such simplified versions were extremely successful and maintained good classical principles in even modest buildings throughout Britain and the USA, for at least 150 years.

Palladio modelled his own book on Serlio, rather than Alberti or other leading theorists. This choice, given the high quality of work he illustrated, started his own rise to fame as initially the most influential architect of the Renaissance (Ackerman 1966). He transformed the image of Venice and was largely responsible for the curiosity of visitors, especially from England in the 18th century, wishing to study the Italian cities. It is interesting that it was not just architectural dilettantes who were attracted by such delights. The great German writer Goethe visited Venice and Rome in 1786. He was enchanted by the buildings but perhaps surprisingly, he already knew what he was expecting to see from more than a passing acquaintance with his own copy of *Quattro Libri* (Boucher 1994). Thomas Jefferson (1743–1826) may have read the original Italian edition in Williamsburg library but he certainly used Leoni's version of the book in a number of his projects, including the famous Rotunda at the University of Virginia (Tavernor 1991). In fact, it was the drawings of the Palladians that enabled him to generate great monuments for a great new nation.

The drawings for this Palazzo show the development and maturing of Palladio's ideas in the context of his growing technical and stylistic mastery; and simultaneously the creation of a type of architecture that would serve as a reference for every future advance. The relationship between the base and upper level indicates Palladio's determination to master the most advanced and significant innovations of contemporary design. Ironically, the sources were drawings that illustrated the grand manner of ancient Tuscan and Roman architecture, which were certainly widely circulated and well-known to him. A visit to Rome in 1541 gave Palladio an immediate experience of the architecture of Donato Bramante (1444–1514) and his followers, but it was not relevant to this design as he learnt all that he needed from drawings (Puppi 1975, Bruschi 1977). This early elevation suggests the influence of his Paduan background as it blends the proportion and details of the Loggia Carnaro with the illustration of a palace façade in Serlio's Book VII. As this was not published until 1575, it is assumed that Palladio had seen a preliminary drawing (Tavernor 1991).

3.6   Elevation Design for Palazzo Civena, Vicenza
Andrea Palladio c. 1540

**3.7   Alternative Design for the Prince's
Lodging, Newmarket Place, London**
Inigo Jones 1619

It was for Charles, Prince of Wales, that
Inigo Jones (1573–1652) designed what
may have been the most important building
in his career, namely the Prince's Lodging.
He received the commission for the
Banqueting House in Whitehall during the
same year. The two are not unconnected in
terms of façade design. The surviving
elevations of the Lodging appear as
preliminary drawings. In the more finished-
looking of the two, Jones turned to the work
of Palladio and Serlio. In this design, there
are no attic windows and the roof is lower,
height being given to the ground floor which
is pierced by tall windows with Serlian
surrounds. Yet, it is the other design that is
so revolutionary. In this alternative design,
height is given to the roof with unusually tall
attic windows. This design is surely one of
the sources of the English Country House.
John Webb (1611–1672) was perhaps a
little excessive in his praise of Jones'
design for the West End of St Paul's
Cathedral in writing that the architect *hath
contracted the envy of all Christendom
upon our nation, for a piece of architecture
not paralleled in these last ages of the
world.*

**3.8   Design for the re-fronting of St
Paul's Cathedral, London**
Inigo Jones 1608

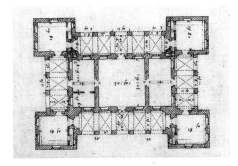

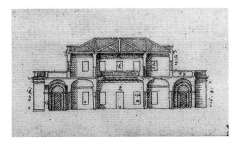

3.9   House with Two Storeys
John Webb c. 1638

Webb's theoretical drawings reflect the response of an architect trained by Jones. The method of presenting the drawings in terms of plan, elevation and section, laid out neatly as if for publication as an engraved sheet, suggests that a treatise was at the back of Webb's mind (Harris 1981). Webb was the nearest that could be attained to a professional architect at that time. When Sir John Denham died in 1669, it might have been expected that he would succeed Denham as Surveyor of The King's Works. It must have caused more than a murmur when this enormously prestigious and influential position went to an academic from Oxford called **Christopher Wren** (1632–1723). Clearly from boyhood to the design of the towers of St Paul's after 1704, Wren liked drawing and was good at it. He retained into his seventies a hand that was orderly, precise, expressive and unshaken. So, it was not an impossible step from drawing mechanisms, dissections and experiments in blood transfusion to a visible realization of architectural ideas. After a chequered period of revival lasting barely twenty-three years, Old St Paul's Cathedral met its fate in the Great Fire of London (1666). Although the façade was left standing, Wren felt unable to incorporate it into his new composition which entailed a complete rebuilding of the Cathedral from the ground upwards (Lees-Milne 1953). He may have been right but it is a familiar story that has accounted for many buildings throughout history to the present day. In 1673, having been encouraged to think more grandly about St Paul's, Wren produced the design recorded by the Great Model (see Figs 9.1, 9.2). After this design had been staked out by the Clergy, he redesigned the Cathedral twice more before work began (Downes 1988). Wren's son records in *Parentalia* that his father wrote *The Architect ought above all things to be well skilled in Perspective.* This is an unexpected statement as there is an absence of perspective drawings from his office. Downes (1988) explains the inconsistency by stating that he was thinking of the ability to visualize rather than draw. Wren continued that even a model is an imperfect guide to what will be built *because a model is seen from other stations and distances than the eye sees the building.* This is true but possibly a surprising observation, given the way that he used models and the kudos that he received from the Great Model of St Paul's, in particular.

**3.10   St Paul's Cathedral, London –
Definitive Design, South Elevation**
Office of Christopher Wren 1675
(see Figs 9.1, 9.2)

Initially St Paul's was not the triumph that might have been supposed. Wren was understandably bitter that the final touches to the cathedral had been taken out of his hands. The early Georgians were not enthused by the architecture but could not ignore it and Wren became famous rather than celebrated. His immediate influence was principally on those he taught, especially Nicholas Hawksmoor (1661–1736), and on the early work of **James Gibbs** (1683–1774), whom he befriended in 1709 when the young Scottish architect arrived in London. In fact Gibbs' steeples exemplified by St Martin's in the Fields, are more directly associated with Wren's designs than are Hawksmoor's towers (Downes 1988). Gibbs even completed the steeple at St Clement Danes, although Wren was still working at the time. He was not a pupil of Wren but was advised by his elder. Gibbs' drawings are superb and clearly impressed Wren who may have thought them better than his own. Moreover Gibbs had received an architectural education from Carlo Fontana in Rome that was vastly more thorough than anything Wren had been able to glean (Little 1975).

**3.11 St Paul's Cathedral, London –
Definitive Design, West Elevation**
Office of Christopher Wren 1675
(see Figs 9.1, 9.2)

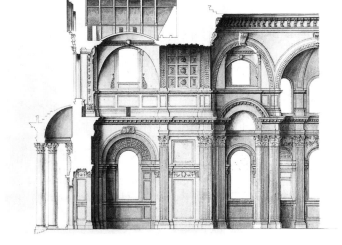

**3.12 St Paul's Cathedral, London –
Definitive Design, Detailed Section**
Office of Christopher Wren 1675
(see Figs 9.1, 9.2)

Gibbs' publication of his drawings in *A Book of Architecture* inspired a number of steeples throughout Europe as well as timber versions in the eastern United States. While there have been fanciful claims that Wren actually designed some of these churches, the source was undoubtedly Gibbs' book (Downes 1988). Before building St Martin's as we know it (see Fig. 9.3), James Gibbs produced two different designs which were rejected by the Committee on grounds of expense. They were both for circular churches evidently derived from a plan in Andrea Pozzo's treatise on perspective, the English edition of which had been published in 1707 by John James. Although these wonderful designs were turned down, Gibbs recorded them in his book commenting that they were more capacious and convenient than the one actually constructed. He encouraged anyone involved in building to reproduce or alter the illustrated designs for their own purposes (Gibbs 1728). The result was that they provided the model for several interesting churches built later in the century – including All Saints by David Stephenson (1786–1796) at Newcastle upon Tyne (Summerson 1991).

3.13 St Martin's in the Fields, London, Circular Church, West Elevation
James Gibbs c. 1718

3.14 St Martin's in the Fields, London, Final Design, North Elevation
James Gibbs c. 1720
(see Fig. 9.3)

There is a general assumption that **William Talman** (1650–1719) was a distinguished court architect as well as owner of exquisite collections of architectural drawings. However, his arrogance resulted in some very dubious decisions and he was extremely ungrateful and antagonistic towards Wren. By 1702, he had a number of successful commissions to his credit but also a number of aggrieved and dissatisfied patrons to his debit (Harris, Soane Gallery Catalogue 1998). He coveted the position as Comptroller of the Royal Works but lost it to Vanbrugh (Whinney 1971, Little 1975). Assessments of the quality of his work are also variable. Wren's office produced a scheme for the proposed Whitehall Palace but the comment that the largest of all the drawings is by William Talman, whose heavy draughtsmanship is singularly unattractive compared with that of Wren (Whinney 1971), seems a little harsh. The aerial perspective for the Trianon is perhaps slightly naïve but it is an interestingly unusual view for its time. The gardens appear stretched out by the asymetric one point perspective technique but otherwise the drawing is well conceived and gives a good impression of the building in its context.

3.15 Unexecuted Design for a Trianon at Thames Ditton
William Talman 1696

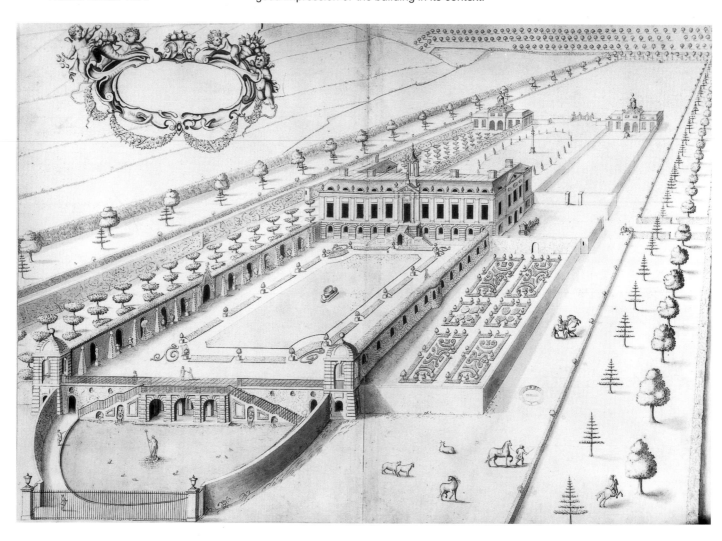

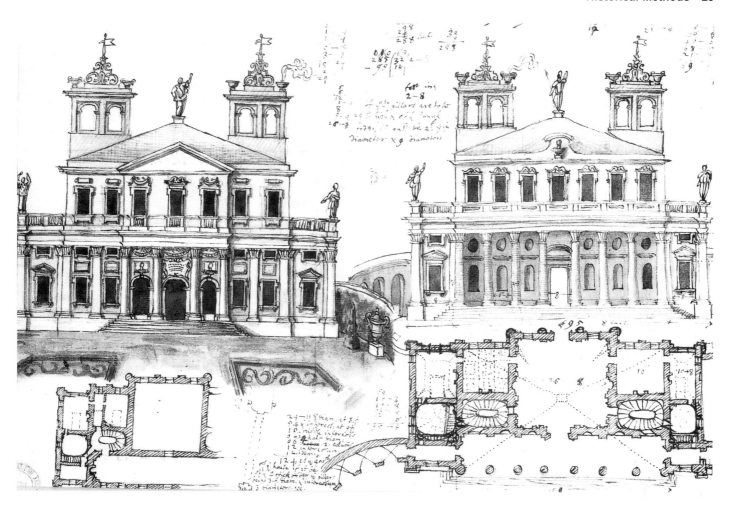

3.16 Design for a Villa near Hampton Court

John Talman 1699

John Talman (1677–1726) was the eldest son of William, who wished John to be his successor. William sent him on many trips abroad to view high quality building design. On some occasions he travelled as a mentor to William Kent. John seems to have enjoyed his role as bon-viveur, connoisseur, guide and collector; deciding not to spoil his life by having to work at designing buildings. He helped out his father with some drawings of proposals in the vicinity of Hampton Court, perhaps to convince the elder that another trip to Europe would further benefit his development. The little design work that he did achieve was rather extravagant and none was built. Yet, this drawing has admirable qualities and there was clearly unfulfilled ability. The freehand representation of plans and elevations brought together in an informal composition has been a constant joy to many observers. Having inherited his father's wealth, he retired to the Shires, only to die himself barely seven years later. Sadly, even his role as guardian of historical drawings is brought into question as John disposed of his father's fabulous collections at the earliest opportunity.

Sciagraphy was generally understood until the end of 17th century as *the art of drawing shadows*. In the 18th and 19th centuries, it also referred to a cut or section of a building (Perez-Gomez and Pelletier 1997). The section drawn in this way is a useful technique for demonstrating the intended interior design and style of décor. Sciagraphy formed the basis of a revolution in drawing, evident in these examples from Campbell and Chambers. Architectural representation became an organized and logical system, based on detailed plans, sections and elevations each with strong shadows. This style was closely coupled to a design process that involved rational planning (Middleton 1982). Both reached their zenith in the Ecole des Beaux-Arts (1819–1968) and this way of drawing became a requirement in nearly all Schools of Architecture until the mid 20th century. Many of the principles can be traced right back to Marcus Vitruvius Pollio, the Roman architect who, in the 1st century BC, was the author of the oldest and most influential work on architecture in existence (Morgan 1914).

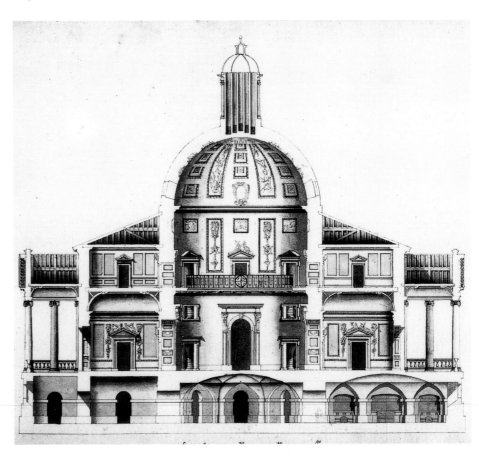

3.17   Design for Mereworth Castle, Kent
Colen Campbell 1720

As the author of *Vitruvius Britannicus* (1715, 1717, 1725) **Colen Campbell** (1676–1729) was able to reproduce architectural drawings that would influence design not only in most of Europe but also North America. He used the books to advertise his own buildings as well. Mereworth was not the first neo-Palladian country house but it was the most closely modelled on a specific prototype – the Villa Capra near Vicenza; also known as the Rotunda (Harris 1972). While the Grand Tour, which incorporated studies of Palladian architecture, was a well-known route for aspiring architects, it is suggested that the accuracy of Mereworth was due to careful examination of Palladio's drawings rather than the building itself. Campbell had already produced a new edition of *Quattro Libri dell' Architettura* (1570) for British consumption in 1716. Certainly Lord Burlington (1694–1753) had access to the drawings of both Palladio and Campbell for his derivative, Chiswick House (1725). The two buildings seem to represent the epitome of English Palladianism, possibly because of the likeness to a real design by Palladio himself. However the style was actually introduced to England by Inigo Jones (Guinness and Sadler 1976).

The sectional design by **William Chambers** (1723–1796) for York House is a development from Campbell's interior and one of the earliest English drawings to show a complete scheme of decoration (Fowler and Cornforth 1978). Chambers produced a *Treatise on Civil Architecture* in 1759 and revised it in 1791. In the book, seven plates are devoted to interior decorative details (Chambers 1791). Both the *Treatise* and the drawing of York House demonstrate a kind of half-way stage in his ideas about interiors. It is interesting that they have the same date, as if Chambers was trying to make a statement about where his work in progress had led him before launching into his fully developed period. As John Harris points out – had the Duke of York built this design, it would have been one of the most striking town houses in London. However, the influence is in the drawing. When exhibited at the Society of Artists in 1761, it would have been given very close attention by visitors ranging from potential clients to fellow architects. The design as expressed by this drawing probably had quite an effect on Robert Adam (1728–1792) who seemingly assimilated parts of it into his own town house designs (Harris 1996).

3.18   Design for York House, Pall Mall, London
William Chambers 1759

William Kent (1685–1748) was first known as a painter and that is how he was described by John Talman during their trips to Italy (Wilson 1984). It has been considered that he had an idiosyncratic and personal style of drawing. The effect is certainly attractive. His treatment of design presentation is in a sense picturesque, achieved by freehand drawing where shadowing conveys depth and reality. Kent may sometimes pencil-in a framework but he also confidently draws freehand in black pen with yellowy brown washes. The finished buildings appear very stiff and serious in comparison with the drawings. The impressions were unique to him and none of his contemporaries adopted his style. Kent himself took until 1725 to establish it. The sources could be that in 1720 it was Lord Burlington who purchased from John Talman his father's collection of designs by Jones and Webb. In 1721, he also managed to acquire Talman's Palladio drawings. Some of Palladio's section drawings are coloured with a brown wash over a black pen outline and shadowed to convey an effect of depth or perspective. By 1723, Burlington had begun using Palladio's drawings as models, and by 1724 he had given Kent the task of preparing the Jones–Webb designs for *The Designs of Inigo Jones with Some Additional Designs, 1727*. The catalyst for his rise to architect from interior designer was undoubtedly the experience of editing this book. Later, Kent used the drawings from the book as source material for his own designs. He prepared these attractive freely-drawn washed sketches for client approval. After agreement had been reached, draughtsmen such as Isaac Ware (1704–1766) would carefully draw them in the proper orthographic manner. What is quite extraordinary is the large number of drawings for the Houses of Parliament that are in Kent's own hand. Clearly, Burlington and Kent regarded this project as the opportunity of a lifetime (Harris, Soane Gallery Catalogue 1998). Despite the assertions that Kent drew more in ink than pencil, his representations maintain a lightness achieved through pencil shading and colour wash. The proposed elevation of the Houses of Parliament is so positively and studiously drawn that it is most likely to be by one of his favoured draughtsmen. The book by Kent's long-time assistant and friend, John Vardy (1718–1765) *Some Designs of Mr Inigo Jones and Mr William Kent* became the latter's final tribute.

3.19   Design for the Rotunda, Carlton Garden, Pall Mall, London
William Kent c. 1733

3.20   Design for the Houses of Parliament, London
Isaac Ware ? for William Kent c. 1735

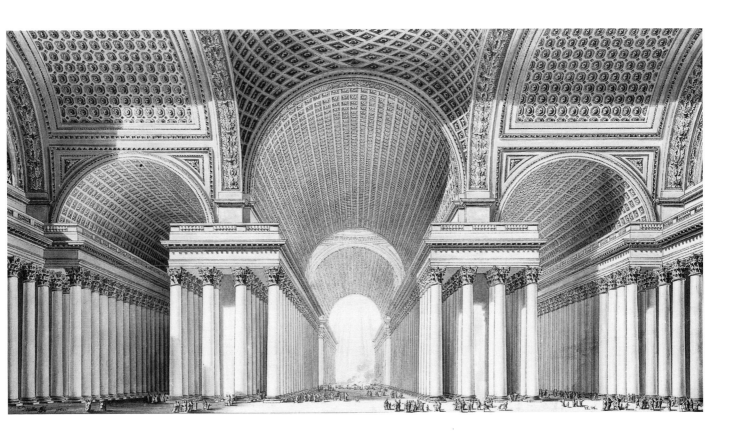

3.21 Design for a Metropolitan Cathedral
Etienne-Louis Boullée 1782

In the mid 18th century, Jean Laurent Legeay (1710–1786) was an important teacher of a whole generation of French architects, including **Etienne-Louis Boullée** (1728–1799). A kindred spirit of Giovanni Battista Piranesi, Legeay maintained that a project is not complete without a rendered perspective view of the whole building. Like Piranesi, Boullée insisted that his architecture was exemplified in perspectives for projects like the Metropolitan Cathedral, rather than in his constructed buildings (Perez-Gomez and Pelletier 1997). Indeed, despite a notable architectural practice in Paris, Boullée was considerably more influential through his writings and drawings than completed work. He dreamt of geometrical architecture that was invariably megalomaniac in effect. In this design, Boullée's stated intention was to produce an impression of overwhelming grandeur (Harris 1972). The massive vaulted ceiling and seemingly endless columns, standing like soldiers, dwarf the gathering below. This is the architecture of power with impact at the time of the French Revolution, and revived during the totalitarian regimes of the early 20th century (Perouse de Montclos 1974).

From the 16th to 18th centuries, architectural drawing developed from being rare and rudimentary to become attractive and quite sophisticated. A small number of very influential publications certainly helped this process. Arguably the most significant were Palladio's *Quattro Libri,* Gibb's *Book of Architecture* and Campbell's *Vitruvius Britannicus*. The opportunity to exhibit architectural drawings also significantly raised the standard. New designs and their presentation were given close scrutiny at the Society of Artists, while the quality displayed at the Royal Academy Summer Exhibition was such that many architects employed artists to illustrate their designs to best advantage. The emphasis of art in architecture led almost directly to the Picturesque Movement which flourished in the 19th century. Grand architecture was displayed in rich paintings. As tastes changed, there became a concern that the artists' impressions were becoming too detached from the reality of the buildings they were intended to illustrate. This led to a movement in which the craftsmanship of buildings became the main feature.

4.0 **Design for the Ballroom at Montagu House, 22 Portman Square, London**
Joseph Bonomi 1790

The Picturesque Movement started in the second half of the 18th century. It first appeared in representations of landscapes but as the new century beckoned, it started to move towards architecture. The Picturesque Architects were particularly inspired by Canaletto, especially after his move to London. It was exciting to be influenced by such great artists, but any architect wishing to become a Royal Academician actually had to exhibit there and would be competing for space with the topographical artists like Joseph Mallord William Turner.

Some architects decided to employ their own artists to give themselves a better opportunity for success but it was not necessarily as easy as that. When **John Soane** (1753–1837) joined Dance's office in the 1780s, he worked alongside Peacock who had just produced a publication stating that flashy perspectives misled clients as to the ultimate appearance of buildings. Soane may have been affected by this viewpoint because as his own master, he would present designs in orthogonal projection supplemented by an elaborate model (see Figs 9.4, 9.5, 9.6).

However, all was to dramatically change when **Joseph Michael Gandy** (1771–1843) joined his office as a paid assistant in 1798. The presentation style became radically altered as Gandy produced a stream of perspectives of Soane's work for the Royal Academy in a style reminiscent of Turner's view of Kirkstall Abbey. This must have represented a huge philosophical upheaval for Soane but he realized the impact on potential clients of exhibiting his designs. It also started to break down the barriers between design illustration and topographical painting. Both types of impression were now on a journey towards a kind of picturesque fantasy.

Gandy had left Soane's office by 1801, although he continued to illustrate the designs. Living in continual poverty, Gandy even drew industriously in Fleet Prison. Between 1798 and 1838, there were only three years that the Royal Academy did not include his name. He showed no fewer than 112 pictures. Gandy started out to be an architect but became more interested in fantasy. He admired the work of **Giovanni Battista Piranesi** (1720–1778) who had attracted some criticism for his approach. A number of architects considered that certain characteristics must be retained in representation to give it credibility as intended architecture. For example, if scale is lost or even rendered ambiguous, drawings become incapable of communication in architectural terms (Summerson 1949). Gandy was heading for a similar difficulty. He did not produce

enough work to be taken seriously as an architect or artist, and his reputation was suppressed by being viewed as an architectural perspectivist. The prevailing opinion was that he needed to generate paintings that were closer to reality. His florid style gave some kind of artistic authority to Soane's rather austere designs but everybody knew that the interior spaces were more accurately depicted by the models than by Gandy's paintings (Richardson 1998). One of the issues raised by Summerson is the value of Gandy to Soane. Gandy was always grateful for the continuous employment, although he lived in poverty. Yet, there is an issue of the fantasies as source material for Soane's designs. Summerson at least hints that Gandy may have been the source of some of his employer's architectural inspiration.

4.1   Design for the Three Per Cent Consol's Office, Bank of England, London

Joseph Michael Gandy for John Soane 1799

(see Figs 9.5, 9.6)

Joseph Gandy may never be placed high among the artists and architects of 19th century England, but in the kingdom of architectural fantasy he reigns absolute. He was the English Piranesi and once launched on a career of draughtsmanship, he never used his drawings to advertise himself as an architect (Summerson 1949). Perhaps he enjoyed the fantasies far more than the reality. When Soane asked him to illustrate the grandeur of the proposed Bank of England in a way that also showed the interior spaces, Gandy turned to Piranesi's work on the ruins of Ancient Rome. It is unclear if there is anything sinister in the depiction of either Soane's design or the Bank of England as a ruin. Sadly, it did actually occur as within a hundred years Soane's building was almost completely swept away to make space for Herbert Baker's redevelopment (see Fig. 9.8). Gandy's painting is a compelling piece of art and arguably one of the pinnacles of 19th century architectural illustration. It represents a building that was yet to be constructed, but it also has the hypnotic qualities that one finds in ancient ruins. Gandy produced numerous examples of visual poetry and this is surely one of his best.

4.2 The Baths of Caracalla
Giovanni Battista Piranesi 1760

4.3 *(overleaf)* **Aerial cutaway view of the Bank of England, London, from the south-east**
Joseph Michael Gandy for John Soane 1830
(see Figs 9.5, 9.6)

The courageous and magnificent design for London's Royal Exchange by **Charles Robert Cockerell** (1788–1863) was a casualty of probably the most notorious of all 19th century architectural competitions. Otherwise it would have easily taken its place near the apex of his achievement. In every way it would have been Cockerell's most personal building. A measure of its meaning to him is suggested by his decision to display his superb wash-drawing for the project directly above his drawing board. As a permanent fixture, it was to find an echo in nearly all his subsequent works (Dodd 1963).

4.4   Competition Design for the Royal Exchange, London
CR Cockerell 1839

4.5   Design for the Great Hall, Scarisbrick, Lancashire
AWN Pugin 1836

The most conspicuous characteristic of Victorian architecture is its diverse use of historic styles. Since architectural development is not a continuum, it is hardly surprising that major influences were inherited from the 18th century in the form of revivals. The inspiration drawn from picturesque values, often reflected in multi-coloured, strongly textured buildings in the spirit of eclecticism, informed its taste for exotic forms of architecture (Palmes 1975). This enabled specialization in a particular style. One of the leading architects of the Gothic Revival was **Augustus Welby Northmore Pugin** (1812–1852). His father, AC Pugin, was principally an architectural draughtsman. AC took on pupils to help him with his volumes on *Specimens of Gothic Architecture*, and soon established a flourishing school of architectural drawing. AWN began work as a precocious young man of fifteen years old. By 1833, he was convinced that Gothic was his only style. His draughtsmanship was fully developed and capable of great complexity. Indeed, it has been argued that his draughtsmanship reached maturity before his architectural style which hung on to the qualities of youthful extravagance and impracticality.

Complementary to his antiquarian studies was AWN's outstanding early work as a decorative artist, where his passionate love for Gothic was united with his great ability to draw. He had an instinctive feeling for linear patterns which he knew how to vary endlessly. These two passions were the reasons for his most important book *Contrasts*, published in 1836. He always needed to understand the structure and appreciate the balance between that structure and ornament. The ability to draw this balance so clearly also gave his designs their strength and conviction (Wedgwood 1998). With his delicate and fluent pen, he easily provided the required Gothic detailing for both Charles Barry and Gillespie Graham in their entries for the competition for the new Palace of Westminster held in 1835. Upon his appointment, Barry at once invited Pugin to join him because he admired Pugin's genius for Gothic detailing, his draughtsmanship and his enthusiasm (Fleetwood-Hesketh 1963) which are all evident in the completed work. AWN's beautiful illustrations showed how deep was his understanding of Gothic construction and ornament and the work of his short life became a model for others to follow (Clark 1963).

George Gilbert Scott (1811–1878) had the biggest practice that any one architect has ever enjoyed in Britain. He had a large office, talented staff and could design some seriously handsome buildings himself. He became President of the Royal Institute of British Architects, Royal Gold Medallist, Professor of Architecture at the Royal Academy, and was widely regarded as the most prolific architect of the century. Scott grew up in a country parsonage, receiving little formal education and nurturing no particular ambition except developing a taste for drawing, like some young lady of a good Victorian family. On this slender basis and with some instruction from a clerical uncle, at sixteen he was articled to an architect who was a shadowy figure in the City of London. However Scott developed a particular skill which catapulted him to greatness. He could design the most beautiful picturesque outlines, as in the much loved St Pancras (Betjeman 1952). The well-managed and expanding Midland Railway had at last attained its own London terminus and in 1865 asked several architects to compete for the design of a station and hotel. Scott's design was for a building of greater bulk and much greater cost than had been envisaged. Nevertheless, it seems that the greater prominence appealed to the Midland Directors and his plans were accepted. Scott designed St Pancras with his own hand and exceptional care. He drew out the elevations and thoughtfully related openings. He then applied the riches of fifty sketchbooks to ornament the construction with 14th century Gothic detail according to his stated philosophy. The result is a building which, had it been his only major work, would have placed him at once among the first half-dozen Victorian architects (Cole 1963). In another notorious architectural competition, rumours abounded that the new Foreign and War Offices were to be built in a classical style. So Scott submitted a scheme mainly in French Gothic, and was consequently placed third. Then the Prime Minister, Lord Palmerston, rejected the first and second prize-winning schemes. The Tory Sub-committee set up to oversee the project were totally bemused by these events and appointed Scott as the architect. The story may appear to be a little disturbing, but in terms of the drawings and eventual building, Scott produced a scheme that has been admired ever since.

4.6 St Pancras Railway Station and Midland Grand Hotel, Euston Road, London
George Gilbert Scott 1865

4.7 Perspective of the Courtyard Side of the Foreign Office, Whitehall, London
George Gilbert Scott 1859

WR Lethaby writes of the mid-Victorian architects *one group turns to imitation, style, effects, paper designs and exhibitions; the other founds on building, on materials and ways of workmanship. One group Betjeman calls the Softs and the other Hards; the former were primarily sketchers and exhibitors of designs, the other thinkers and constructors.* A definite *hard* was **Alfred Waterhouse** (1830–1905) whose best works were undoubtedly Manchester Town Hall and the Assize Courts depicted by several versions of this lavish rendering. Like the other *hards*, he thought in Gothic (Betjeman 1952).

Waterhouse is also much remembered for the Natural History Museum in South Kensington. By March 1868, he had succeeded in the formidable task of virtually redesigning Fowke's building on the allocated site in South Kensington. Yet, a number of people may not be acquainted with this perspective of the Museum for a different site. The new First Commissioner had visions of an even more grand metropolitan development, and wanted the design transposed to the Embankment. Waterhouse was so pressed for time that he could do little more to adapt his design to the new curved site than bend the façade, while he continued with his work at Manchester. It may have been a rushed job at the time but the movement and fluidity in this drawing produce an exciting contrast to his more formal presentation drawings. He developed the scheme no further, as by 1870, the old site was back in favour again (Cunningham and Waterhouse 1992). Unfortunately the Assize Courts were damaged by bombing in the Second World War and later demolished but the Town Hall and Natural History Museum still stand as testaments to his genius. Particularly moving is the quality of spaces generated by the Gothic structure.

4.8   Manchester Assize Courts
Alfred Waterhouse 1859

4.9   Preliminary Perspective of the Natural History Museum, London
Alfred Waterhouse 1869

4.10   Interior View of St Mary's, Studley Royal, North Yorkshire

Axel Haig for William Burges 1872

William Burges (1827–1881) was an early and eccentric *hard* who built a medieval world around himself, of jokes and pet animals, but he was also a sound constructor (Betjeman 1952). There remains an enormous collection of Burges' own drawings and sketches, also dozens of notebooks and tiny albums which offer a close view of the way he set out his work. Certainly, he could draw with great precision and many of his sketches show Pre-Raphaelite influences. This is not surprising as several of them, including Rossetti, were among his friends.

Although some of Burges' competition drawings include a few touches of the archaic, they are at the same time simple, informative, and without prettifying deceptions. It is perhaps from the pages of Villard de Honnecourt that he borrowed the trick of including in his drawings, small figures in medieval dress because he believed that every architect should be able to draw the human figure. A dislike of what he called the *scribble style* of drawing went hand in hand with his mistrust of picturesque effects on the drawing board. He criticized AWN Pugin because he *made things look too well by his marvellous etching*, and noted an *action in all his plates which you look for in vain in the real thing.* Burges was no admirer of paper architecture. *What a pity*, he was supposed to have said of his colleague GE Street, *that he cannot build his cross-hatching* (Shaw and Jackson 1892; Blomfield 1912). Yet despite all the pronouncements about architectural drawing, not only did Burges ask the German, Axel Haig to illustrate St Mary's but turned to him again to produce the grand overall effect of the design for the Law Courts (Hitchcock 1958).

Nevertheless, it was **George Edmund Street** (1824–1881) who won the competition. Richard Norman Shaw wrote of him that *the charm of his work is that you may be certain it is entirely his own and this applies to the smallest detail as to the general conception. I am certain that during the whole time I was with him, I never designed a single moulding* (Shaw and Jackson 1892). Augustus W Turner recalled in the *British Architect* of 1 December 1882, that *he used a black ebony engineers' T-square and when drawing, the rattling of this square was incessant.*

4.11   Competition Design for the Royal Courts of Justice, London
Axel Haig for William Burges 1866

4.13   Elevation for the Royal Courts of Justice, London
George Edmund Street 1874

This competition also allows us to view another dimension of Waterhouse's presentational skills.

4.12   Competition Design for the Royal Courts of Justice, London.
Alfred Waterhouse 1866

Street's industry was matched by his severity and self-confidence; he could hardly have been a likeable man. However, he attracted high quality staff. William Morris and Philip Webb both worked in his office. The latter was succeeded as chief draughtsman by Norman Shaw, who added that *the rapidity and precision with which he drew were marvellous . . . When a new work appeared, his custom was to draw it out in pencil in his room – plans, elevations and sections, even putting in the margin lines and places where he wished the title to go; nothing was sketched in, it was drawn exactly as he wished it to be, so that there was little to do except to ink in his drawings to complete them* (Kinnard 1963). **Richard Norman Shaw** (1831–1912) had an enormous influence on domestic architecture. He and Morris might equally be described as founders of the Arts and Crafts Movement (Betjeman 1952). Shaw's father had been a military man, then a painter of watercolours and then the leading formal gardener of the day. The son was a brilliant draughtsman too. He learnt the skill from **JD Harding** (1798–1863) who also taught John Ruskin (Pevsner 1963).

4.14   Design for Leyswood, Groombridge, Sussex
Richard Norman Shaw 1868

4.15 Bird's Eye View of the Crystal Palace and the Grounds at Sydenham, Kent
JD Harding for Joseph Paxton 1854

In the second half of the 19th century, new trends in British architecture were increasingly centred around domestic work and relied much on the picturesque approach, even though some of the pioneers came from the Gothic Revival tradition. These were architects who had learned how to express the three dimensionality of buildings forcefully, who knew about modelling and truth to materials but also had powers of observation developed by studying Gothic precedent (Shaw 1858). **Ernest George** (1839–1922) was a particularly skilled watercolourist who undertook regular continental tours and returned with sketchbooks full of architectural references upon which he could base his own designs. To represent his buildings, George favoured soft edges. This is in contrast to Shaw who developed a pen technique that avoided variations in tone. The black and white nature of these drawings was particularly appropriate to the new printing techniques. The ease with which impressions could be reproduced, together with the Olde English fantasies that his designs represented, meant that Shaw was in great demand by editors of magazines such as *Country Life*. Attendant publicity enabled him to become well known amongst a wide readership which included a number of future clients. Ernest George was certainly capable of making exquisite line sketches washed in sepia that seemed to portray delightful old houses. The ancient character was so well established in silhouette and massing that the eye took for granted a similar character in the architectural detail and texture of the materials, even though actually there was only the vaguest indication of what those would be. The charm of these sketches became legendary (Goodhart-Rendel 1963). When **Edwin Lutyens** (1869–1944) started to work for himself in about 1890, English architecture was arguably reaching its highest peak, The masters of the Gothic, like Waterhouse and Street, had done their work. Philip Webb and Norman Shaw were still designing houses and the self-assured younger architects included CFA Voysey and Ernest Newton. Charles Rennie Mackintosh would win the Glasgow School of Art competition at the age of 28, and Giles Gilbert Scott would win the Liverpool Anglican Cathedral competition at 23. It appeared that everyone was young and the course of English architecture seemed clear (Gradidge 1976).

4.16 Design for 50 and 52 Cadogan Square, London
Ernest George 1885

In the years immediately following his apprenticeship, the principal conscious influence on **Charles Francis Annesley Voysey** (1857–1941) was Norman Shaw. He also had a very great respect for the ability of Lutyens, and admired the work of Ruskin and Pugin's Gothic. Voysey wrote that *you may search the Houses of Parliament from top to bottom and you will not find one superficial yard that is copied from any pre-existing building.* With the help of his friend Arthur Mackmurdo, Voysey obtained income as a pattern designer of wallpapers and woven fabrics. He was successful but it did not satisfy him. He wanted to build, and as a start he designed a small house for himself and his future wife – hoping to persuade a wealthy friend to finance it. The scheme fell through and the house was never built, but in 1888 the drawings were published in *The Architect* and caught the eye of MH Lakin who gave Voysey his first important commission. Gradually other work followed. Like Street, Voysey designed every detail himself and his pupils or assistants had little to do but to make the necessary copies. When illustrations of his work began to appear in the architectural papers and in *The Studio*, they were eagerly awaited and collected by architectural students all over Europe. His

influence in Austria, Germany and Scandinavia was considerable. John Betjeman is reported to have asked FH Newberry, who taught Charles Rennie Mackintosh and later commissioned him to design the Glasgow School of Art, how his former pupil gained his inspiration. Apparently Newberry cited the published drawings of Voysey as a major influence. It is sad that Voysey did not repay the compliment, especially as there are similarities in their house designs. He disliked any architecture which in his view turned away from *the spiritual something given to the development of traditional forms by the individual artist* (Brandon-Jones 1963). The substantial collection of Voysey's drawings at the RIBA Drawings Collection as well as those in the Victoria and Albert Museum demonstrate that he was the sole designer of his buildings. However, the famous perspective watercolours are by Howard Gaye. They were primarily intended for Royal Academy Summer Exhibitions but would have been very persuasive in presenting the design to a client. Evidence from Voysey's visits to Windermere shows that the watercolours were undertaken during the design phase. He paid Gaye two guineas for the now priceless perspective of Broadleys. Gaye

4.17 Preliminary Design for the Ferry Inn at Rosneath, Dumbartonshire, Scotland
Edwin Lutyens 1896

does not appear on Voysey's list of pupils but seems to have been engaged separately for the projects to make a perspective of each. In the Batsford Gallery Exhibition of 1931, Voysey made it clear that of the twenty perspectives exhibited, fifteen were by Howard Gaye and the remaining five were his own drawings (Hitchmough 1995). A typical watercolour of a Voysey house is Gaye's depiction of Greyfriars, on the Hog's Back, near Puttenham, Surrey. It is assumed that the model for the sheet layout was determined by Voysey. As in this case, they all have one or two perspectives, plans and a pronounced title – all on one sheet. The drawing of Lodge Style at Combe Down is a late example of the technique that Voysey employed throughout his working life. His presentations were mainly in orthogonal projection with the various components arranged on the sheet as if he were designing one of his many patterns.

4.18   Presentation Drawing for Greyfriars Puttenham, on the Hog's Back, Surrey
Howard Gaye for CFA Voysey 1897

4.19   Preliminary Design for Lodge Style, Combe Down, near Bath
CFA Voysey 1909

A fine draughtsman and architect, **Arthur Beresford Pite** (1861–1934) won the Soane Medallion in 1882 with his design for *A West End Club House* in what might be called Wagnerian Romantic style. He also redesigned the West End to go with it. At the other end of the scale, **Charles Rennie Mackintosh** (1869–1928) went in search of extreme simplicity and built The Hill House in a Beardsleyesque Scottish Baronial style at Helensburgh. During the 19th century, architectural drawing of various kinds reached a level in terms of quality and diversity that may have been surpassed in individual cases at other times but probably not in terms of universal output. Every leading architect had a pocket-sized sketchbook and a set of watercolours. In the early part of the 20th century, a significant change began to spread through the English architectural scene. The reasons were varied and numerous but not least amongst them was the increasing influence from America. It spelt the end, at least for many decades, of the English picturesque tradition and laid the path for the eventual acceptance of continental modernism (Fellows 1998).

4.20 Competition Design for a West End Club, London.
Arthur Beresford Pite 1882

4.21 The Hill House, Helensburgh, Dumbartonshire
Charles Rennie Mackintosh 1903

Until the beginning of the 20th century, the only architecture seriously studied outside this country by British architects was the Renaissance in Italy. During the early years of the century, an American architect called Frank Lloyd Wright began to excite British designers with fascinating new forms. In his early years Wright was sceptical if not scathing about what he called pretty perspectives. His designs were dependent on accurate geometry which was worked out in two dimensional drawings before the overall forms were tested by three dimensional representations. Plans have always been fundamental to the organization of building designs. The clarity demanded by two dimensional representations enabled plans, sections and elevations to be precisely drawn and laid out next to one another. Even competitions started to favour this kind of presentation in an attempt to discover a new realism. Evolving structural designs enabled more interesting vertical relationships between spaces, and sections through the intended buildings became increasingly significant in expressing the ideas. Meanwhile, the use of glass in building envelopes enabled modern architecture to appear as structure in space.

5.0 North Elevation for the Church at Prinknash Abbey, Cranham, Gloucestershire
HS Goodhart-Rendel c. 1953

Chapter 5 **Two Dimensional Drawings**

Charles Reilly wrote in the *Manchester Guardian* during 1931 that **Cyril Arthur Farey** (1888–1954) *is the chief exponent today of modern architectural draughtsmanship in this country, and one of the best of our modern architectural critics.* Farey was awarded the Sir William Tite (1798–1873) prize for the study of Italian Renaissance Architecture in 1913 and received the Soane Medallion for architectural drawing less than a year later. He was also a Gold Medallist of the Royal Academy Schools and exhibited there on numerous occasions, where his beautiful renderings were much admired.

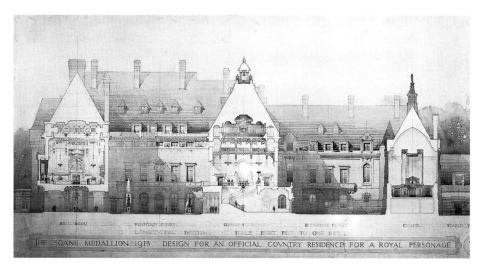

5.1   Sectional Elevation of the Official Country Residence for a Royal Personage
Cyril Farey 1913

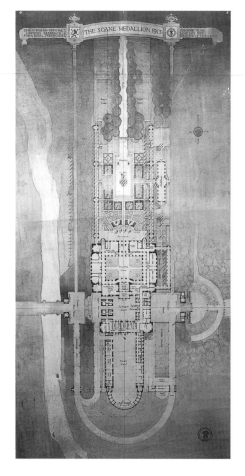

5.2   Ground Plan of the Official Country Residence for a Royal Personage
Cyril Farey 1913

5.3   Elevation of the Guggenheim Museum, New York
Frank Lloyd Wright c. 1944
(see Fig. 6.4)

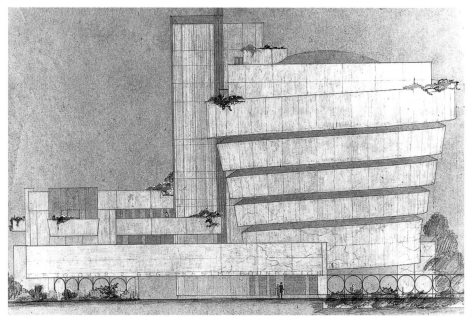

Although coloured pencils were probably the favourite medium of **Frank Lloyd Wright** (1867–1959), for the Guggenheim Museum, he seems to have chosen exclusively white chalk and pencil shading. The essence of its concept is the spiral and there are many elevations and sections showing slightly different versions of it. Drexler (1962) claims that by the middle of the 20th century few architects relied on perspective drawings for any purpose more serious than to sell the building to the client, which is serious enough, and few architects had the time or inclination to draw. Wright clearly did have the time and inclination to draw. The photographs of him at the board with groups of students around him are surely not for effect. The Taliesin archives hold an estimated 8000 drawings. These are records of some of the greatest buildings of modern times in the world, and fascinating to students, architects and the public. For much of his life, Wright was sceptical about *pretty perspectives*. Even after he accepted them as a legitimate means of testing the building design, he still worked out the geometry in orthogonal projection (Wright 1932).

Wright was renowned for being pungently critical of all architectural work that did not meet with his approval. Towards the end of his life he visited a remote village in North Wales and **Clough Williams-Ellis** (1883–1978) wrote in *Portmeirion: the Place and its Meaning* (1963) how Wright had been captivated by it. He may have recognized in Williams-Ellis another personification of rebellion against the conformity and dullness of the modern age. The playfulness, highly individual buildings, picturesque conjunctions and the feeling of organic growth would all have been familiar to him. Portmeirion

opened in 1926 and was developed by Williams-Ellis right up to his death in 1978. This drawing is considered by Haslam (1996) to be of utmost importance, as it is the earliest surviving representation of his vision for a group of structures adapted to a breathtakingly beautiful natural coastline. He feels that it shows the architect thinking aloud about towers for bells, the irregularity of plan form reminiscent of centuries of development on the Italian coastline and he refers to the concept of architecture as a mediating element between sea and land, both visually and functionally.

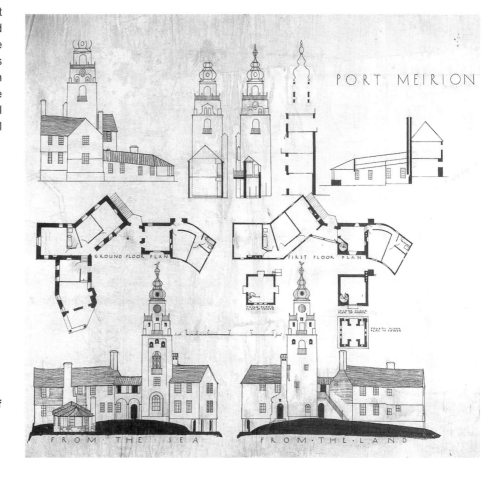

5.4   Plans and Elevations for a Group of Buildings with Campanile at Portmeirion, Gwynedd
Clough Williams-Ellis 1925

Some observers have pointed to associations between Richmond Riverside and Portmeirion. Amazingly, this is seen by some as a kind of criticism whereas it should be seen as an enormous compliment. **Quinlan Terry** (b 1937) had been a dissatisfied and unhappy assistant when he was introduced to Raymond Erith (1904–1973) who had a small practice in rural north east Essex. Soon Terry joined him in partnership and learnt much from their close working relationship. Erith's admiration for Soane and Palladio was particularly good detailed material but Terry's most dramatic development came in 1967 with the opportunity to measure buildings in Rome, on a scholarship. He assembled the drawings into an unpublished album called the *Roman Sketchbook* which contains a huge variety of buildings. Despite accusations to the contrary, Terry is eager to experiment with ideas from his sketchbooks and other sourcebooks, that he has not tried before (Aslet 1986). A long term derelict site in a highly desirable location next to the Thames at Richmond has provided the practice with their biggest opportunity to date. Although essentially a group of speculative offices, the composition of well-conceived buildings and spaces offers a real contribution to the town. The drawings are also beautifully conceived. They are mainly in orthographic projection with a shaded pencil technique that is a reminder of Frank Lloyd Wright. The attention to detail ensures that both the buildings and the drawings come alive. One of the charms of the restaurant elevation is the way in which the sheet becomes part of the drawing. The inset plan and elevation are evident in a number of high quality historical precedents.

5.5   Restaurant Building Elevation at Richmond Riverside, Surrey
Quinlan Terry 1987
(see Figs 6.0, 9.26)

5.6   (opposite) Sketch View of Worcester College, Oxford
MacCormac Jamieson Pritchard 1980
(see Fig. 9.25)

At Worcester College, Oxford, by **MacCormac** (b 1938) **Jamieson** (b 1939) and **Pritchard** (b 1948) the history is re-interpreted but it is the fascinating composition of buildings and spaces that is crucial to the scheme. Arguably, the setting is not strongly expressed in the drawings. They mainly focus on the three dimensional spatial relationships. The sketch view shows the attractive form and massing of the proposed development whereas the plan and view from provost garden are more demonstrative of organizational aspects in the design.

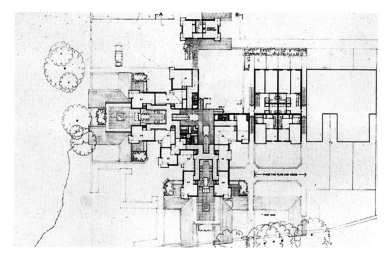

5.7   Plan of Worcester College, Oxford
MacCormac Jamieson Pritchard 1980
(see Fig. 9.25)

5.8   View from Provost's Garden, Worcester College, Oxford
MacCormac Jamieson Pritchard 1980
(see Fig. 9.25)

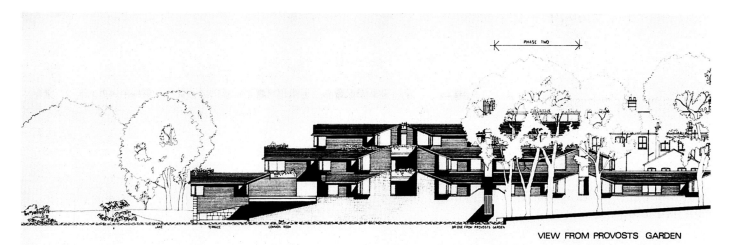

VIEW FROM PROVOSTS GARDEN

The competition entry by **Barry Gasson** (b 1935) with Cambridge University colleagues John Meunier and Britt Andreson for the Burrell Collection in Glasgow, was less concerned with a specific building than with evoking the spirit of the museum that they wanted to build. They included dramatic montages of the woods and the concept was based on a walk in the park (AR February 1984). The assessors' reaction was that during the first phase it appeared in a somewhat thin and tentative format but had emerged as a richly worked out and extremely elegant solution (AJ 22 March 1972). The plan shows a high degree of geometrical organization with the solidity of the building towards its core. In terms of both the drawing and reality, this allows for a contrast with the thin glazed screen that invites the woods into the exhibition. The effect is emphasized by the angle of the screen which follows the edge of the woods and cuts across the disciplined three dimensional grid. Meunier and Andreson left to take up other posts before the building began on site. It took Gasson twelve rather lonely years to complete. He abandoned architecture as a career shortly afterwards and now lives in France.

5.9   Ground Floor Plan of the Burrell Collection, Glasgow
Barry Gasson 1971
(see Fig. 9.22)

Hugh Casson (1910–1999) and **Neville Conder** (b 1922) produced a completely different kind of solution to their parkland setting. The Elephant and Rhinoceros House occupies an island site near the southern boundary of the Zoological Gardens in Regents Park. Elephants are such architectural animals that there is a temptation to look at a building which houses them as a kind of analogy. Indeed this design can be described in terms of its massive curves, wrinkled hide and curious silhouette. The pictorial resemblance to the elephant image is evident in the drawing. There is an element of deliberate fantasy about a bunch of rounded bodies with their heads in the air. In fact, it is a synthesis of the fantastic and the functional. This highly stylized drawing accurately depicts the strongly artificial building style. However, there could be a debate about the appropriateness as informality and naturalistic impressions are often the principal aims in such circumstances. Moreover, the main characteristic of an elephant is its size. Yet, the bulk and scale of this building, with its huge concrete ribs, actually makes the animals look quite small (AR July 1965).

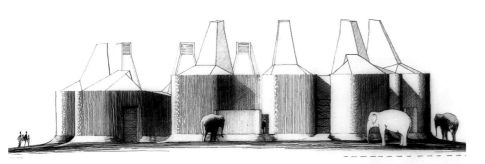

**5.10 Final Revised Elevation of the
Elephant and Rhinoceros House
for the Zoological Society, London**
Hugh Casson and Neville Condor
1964

**5.11 Part Elevation of Competition Entry
for Churchill College, Cambridge**
Howell Killick Partridge and
Amis 1959
(see Fig. 6.8)

Another practice to celebrate the use of concrete as a building material was **Howell** (1922–1974) **Killick** (1924–1971) **Partridge** (b 1924) and **Amis** (b 1924). All four original partners belonged to the first generation of post-war architects and, as such, had their roots firmly embedded in the modern movement. Nevertheless, there were other influences at work. WG Howell's interest in William Burges led him to discover that conscientious detailing invariably produces fine quality (AR January 1951). Howell adopted a similar philosophy and the level of detailed consideration is shown in the drawings. The competition for Churchill College, Cambridge, was actually won by Sheppard Robson and Partners but the HKPA entry is a spectacular essay in angular geometry. There are references to Beaux Arts design in much of their work and although there was a perspective by Barbara Jones, much of the strength of this design is illustrated by the amazingly long orthogonal drawings of elevations wrapping around two five-sided courtyards. The three dimensional modelling of the façades is demonstrated by careful pencil shading (HKPA 1981).

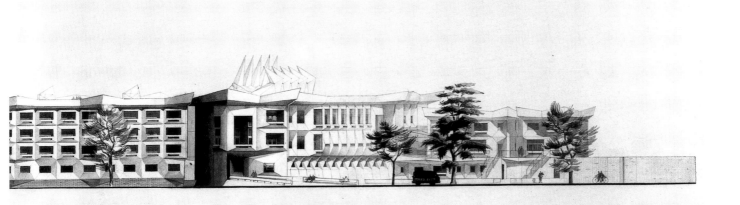

Ahrends (b 1933) **Burton** (b 1933) and **Koralek** (b 1933) were themselves influenced by HKPA, and especially by John Killick who taught them at the Architectural Association in London during the 1950s. There is a brutalist flavour in their early work but generally ABK were more taken with the *unfashionable* Frank Lloyd Wright and his mentor Louis Sullivan. The winning entry for the international competition to design a new library for Trinity College, Dublin, was primarily by Paul Koralek. The partners used it as a basis to set up their practice. Explicitly stated in the brief was the requirement that the new building should represent the 20th century in the way that the College's earlier buildings represented the 18th and 19th centuries (ABK 1991). The solution is one of elegant simplicity that gives a more friendly face to the modern movement. Architectural competitions do not always have such happy endings (Emanuel 1994). The elevations are shown in the context of the adjacent buildings as rectilinear volumes. Three dimensional modelling is an important quality of this design and it is emphasized by strong pencil shading.

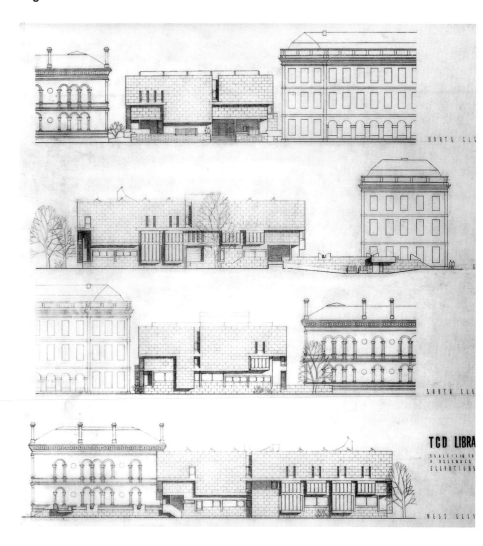

5.12   Elevations of Trinity College, Dublin

Ahrends Burton Koralek 1960

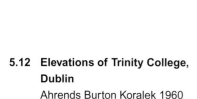

Another of John Killick's students was **Peter Cook** (b 1936). He was a founder member of the Archigram Group London, in 1962 and co-edited the Archigram magazine from 1961 to 1970. The notion of a project, as opposed to a design for a specific building, has a long historical pedigree. It is only during periods of emphasis on practical outcomes that it has been pushed into the background. The drawings for a project of this kind can be inventive, exciting, near the cutting edge of ideas and can go far beyond the limits of construction. As a trade in ideas, the project becomes a means of broadening the architectural debate. Unfortunately, the design of a house as an abstract or philosophical concept can be a little inaccessible for those who are used to a clever plan or pretty elevation (Cook and Llewellyn-Jones 1991). Peter Cook has attained a timeless quality or even a brand of immortality within his own lifetime through drawings and models. His fame as an architect is based on graphics and representations of buildings. As demonstrated by Piranesi and arguably Gandy, this is no bar to immortality. The concept of a project can actually last longer than a completed building.

It is only since his partnership with **Christine Hawley** (b 1949) that Cook has started to concentrate on designs that could be built. At Lutzowplatz in Berlin, the illustrated west elevation to the apartments is open and exuberant, welcoming the evening sun. By contrast the east elevation, which provides light to the bedrooms and bathrooms, is rational and protective (Cook 1990). While drawings of theoretical projects are outside the scope of this book, the Centre Pompidou is generally regarded as the built symbol of Archigram. An international competition launched in 1970 attracted 681 entries. It was won by **Richard Rogers** (b 1933) and **Renzo Piano** (b 1937). The section clearly shows the concept of the building's two layered façades between which are hung a series of open floors and that the façades are in reality deep zones for servicing and movement respectively (Powell 1999). The presentation has distinct references to the 1969 Instant City by Ron Herron (1930–1994), another Archigram member, and the colours and expression of the section are clearly derived from the 1964 Plug-in City by Peter Cook.

5.13 **West Elevation of Lutzowplatz Housing, Berlin**
Cook and Hawley 1984

5.14 *(overleaf)* **Section of Centre Georges Pompidou, Paris**
Piano and Rogers 1971
(see Fig. 9.23)

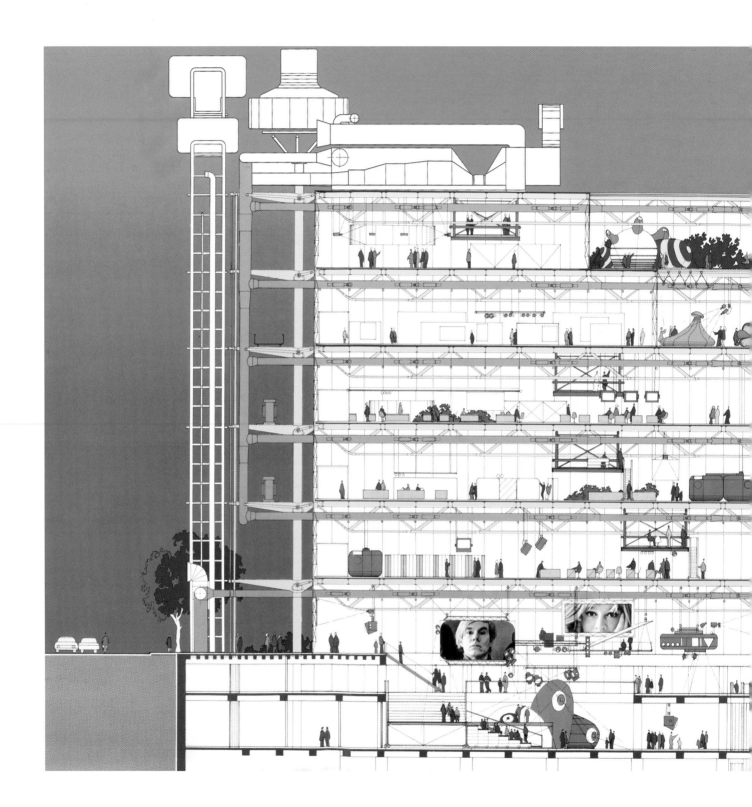

Interests of the **Richard Rogers Partnership** in prefabrication, the impermanence of Constructivist buildings, and Archigram, are all reflected in the Lloyds Building (Powell 1999). Similarities in form and depiction between Lloyds and the 1962 Metal Cabin Housing by Peter Cook (Archigram Exhibition 1994) are really quite startling. The section displays similarities with both Pompidou and the Hong Kong and Shanghai Bank (Foster Associates 1979). Like the former, the structure and services are at the perimeter and similar to the latter, there is a large atrium at the core.

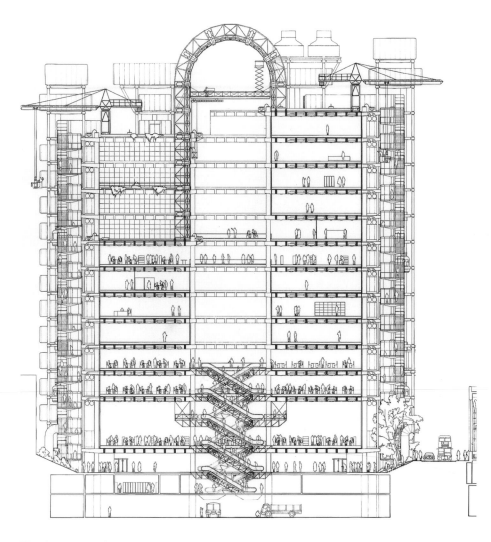

5.15 Short Section, Lloyds of London
Richard Rogers Partnership c. 1980
(see Figs 6.12, 9.24)

Michael Wilford is unusual among architects, with his detailed analysis of the drawings produced by **James Stirling** (1926–1992) **Michael Wilford** (b 1938) **and Associates**. He notes that the appearance of their drawings is deliberately hard, spare, restrained and scientific in character, meticulously to scale and as accurate as hand and eye can make them. According to Wilford, they are meant to convey information clearly and with immediacy. For clarity, it is necessary to omit much information from the drawing and retain it in the mind's eye.

The image on the paper represents the absolute minimum necessary to convey the maximum amount of useful information about the design. He confirms that the process of stripping away extraneous information is done by overlaying tracing paper on an underdrawing and re-drawing it, often many times, until the scope and detail are pared down as required. They use the smallest sheets of paper possible so that the eye can encompass the whole image without any need to scan and search across the page. Apparently, this also eliminates the temptation to incorporate irrelevant information. The design process begins with a series of alternative conceptual studies, and when a single concept has been agreed with the client, they develop a full range of plans, sections, elevations etc. Drawings start as pencil underlays using graphite leads in clutch pencils and as they become finalized, change to Rotring black ink on tracing paper or film. Wilford does not subscribe to the benefits of new technology. Instead, he points out that all the staff are creative architects who think and invent as they draw. The assertion seems to be that CAD usurps the thinking process, rather than just being another tool.

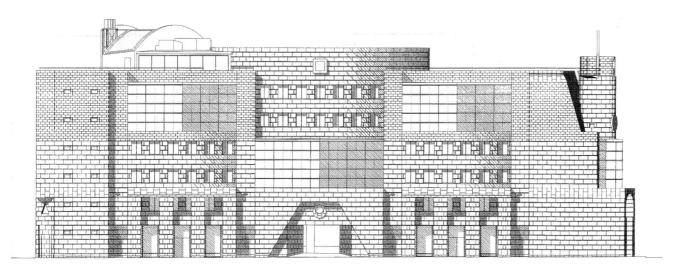

5.16 Elevation to Queen Victoria Street No. 1 Poultry, London
James Stirling Michael Wilford and Associates 1986
(see Figs 6.9, 10.23)

By remaining strictly within the limits of this shared discipline of drawing, they find that the individual creativity of each architect can be expressed far more effectively and comprehensibly to the others because they are all communicating in the same visual language (Wilford, Muirhead, Maxwell 1994). This is a very logical and objective approach to drawing that strongly emphasizes the importance of drawings in communicating design intentions. Yet, there are slight feelings of the kind of mechanical process that they are trying so hard to avoid.

An alternative approach is presented by Nic Sampson. At **Terry Farrell (b 1938) and Partners**, great importance is also attached to the exploration of ideas and to this end considerable responsibility is vested in the drawing. However the difference is that although a successful drawing is a fusion of ideas that establishes its authority in an artistic as well as constructional sense, they claim that it should also be an indulgence and an opportunity to begin a journey without necessarily knowing the destination. They believe that *loose drawing* can help define the brief and encourage lateral thought. It

is a time-consuming and very demanding process where the author of a drawing has the responsibility of locking it into the greater thought-pattern that shapes the design. Embedded within the work is a strong sense of achievability, which may be realistic or artistic. Of all those involved in the building process, the architect is perhaps alone in believing that the drawing has some value over and above its literal role that ultimately leads to construction. In some ways the character of the drawing can anticipate or establish the demeanour of the finished building itself (Latham, Swenarton, Sampson

1998). It is often asked how architects obtain work. Almost regardless of the buildings they represent, Terry Farrell and Partners are able to show any potential clients a fascinating array of illustrations. The variety of style and media in the drawings does not diminish the consistency of output but adds to the scope of future possibilities. They also demonstrate a richness in diversity that must offer the architects in this practice an opportunity to express their individual personalities. The suggestion that the practice has moved from high-tech to post-modern is just too simplistic.

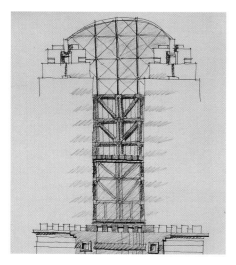

5.17   Concept Sketch Elevation, Lee House, Alban Gate, London
Terry Farrell and Partners 1987
(see Figs 6.13, 8.19)

5.18   West Wing West Elevation, Lee House, Alban Gate, London
Terry Farrell and Partners 1987
(see Fig. 6.13)

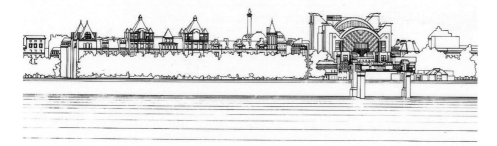

5.19   River Elevation with context, Charing Cross Embankment Place, London
Terry Farrell and Partners 1987
(see Figs 6.14, 9.27)

Farrell's erstwhile partner, **Nicholas Grimshaw** (b 1939), has continued with a high-tech philosophy. An accusation that his designs are cold and obsessed with technique is rather harsh. The suggestion that they are in the tradition of Paxton and Brunel certainly has more appeal, and an observation that the components are articulated like vertebrae (Hellman 2000) has particular resonance. Like a number of successful modern British architects, Grimshaw is a graduate from the AA and some of his early work could well have been inspired by Archigram.

At Waterloo, a distinct identity appropriate to the first monument of a new railway age was especially sought by the clients. Contrary to the much heralded notion that its architects are obsessed by the machine aesthetic, the work of Nicholas Grimshaw & Partners seems to invite imagery from the natural world. An aerial view of the International Terminal has been called a caterpillar eating into the leaf of the station and also as the backbone of Waterloo (AR September 1993). The first of these metaphors confirms that the building is recognized by its roof form and the second is evident in the concept sketch. An initial

theme seems to have been a structural concept generated by jointed vertebrae bending over the trains and people. The asymmetric arch of the roof appears in many of the drawings and much of the scheme is explained through its cross-sections. The curved trusses punctuating the transparent membrane over this Terminal have produced one of the symbols of modern architecture in London. There is even a notion that the architects feel images associated with the roof have become overstated, at the expense of other design issues such as elegant solutions to complex movement patterns.

5.20 Concept Sketch Section, International Terminal, Waterloo, London
Nicholas Grimshaw & Partners
c. 1988
(see Fig. 9.28)

5.21 Cross Section, International Terminal, Waterloo, London
Nicholas Grimshaw & Partners
c. 1988 (see Fig. 9.28)

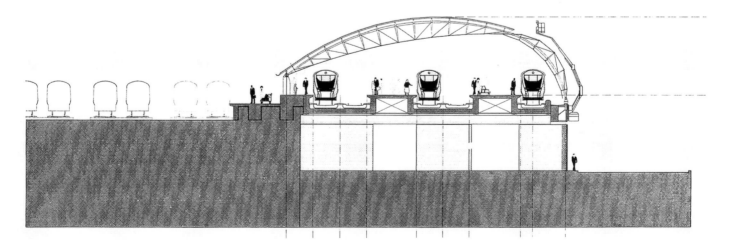

While plans, sections and elevations became quite favoured ways of expressing modern architecture, three dimensional representations were still ever present. It is possibly arguable that they were more functional than the lavish paintings of the 19th century and the architects were demonstrably trying to avoid accusations of deception or seduction in their presentations. The sketch perspective became a well used technique. There was also a move to more rational three dimensional drawings that had their origins in engineering. The axonometric and isometric became almost synonymous with frame and panel architecture. At the same time, the sectional perspective appeared to be based on construction. Towards the end of the 20th century, CAD modelling was used for numerous formal presentations. The technique had developed well beyond its familiar block modelling to a level of great sophistication. The rendering and detail became phenomenal but the equipment remained quite expensive and the quantity of input data required took time to develop. The sketch perspective continued as a more low key, user friendly alternative.

6.0   View across the river, Richmond Riverside, Surrey
Quinlan Terry 1987
(see Figs 5.5, 9.26)

Although beginning his life in the middle of the 19th century, **Frank Lloyd Wright** pioneered and remained fascinated by one of the symbols of 20th century modernism – the system built house. He introduced the Usonian Houses in timber and concrete, many examples of which were constructed in different parts of the USA. He produced designs for the City Block House as a prototype in concrete but the numerous proposals for the All Steel Houses in Los Angeles are amongst some of his most enduring images (Riley, Reid 1994). In his autobiography (1932) Wright commented on the design method of his early employer Joseph Lyman Silsbee, that *he got a ground-plan and made his pretty sketch . . . It would then come out into the drawing room . . . keeping the floor plan near the sketch if possible . . .* However, by the time of the Robie House, Wright had moved closer to Silsbee's method than he perhaps could have imagined. Previously Wright had claimed that no man ever constructed a building worthy of the name of architecture by modelling the plan on a perspective sketch fantasy. He had felt that such methods only produce scene paintings.

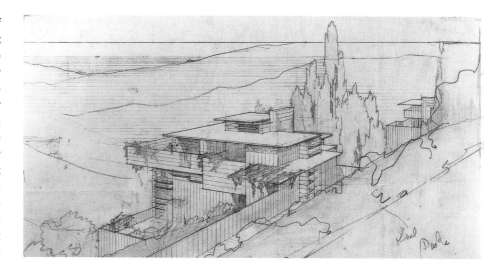

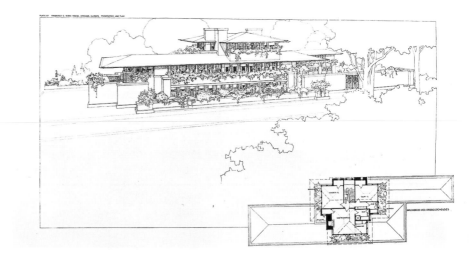

6.1   Perspective, All Steel Houses (unbuilt)
John H Howe for Frank Lloyd Wright 1937

6.2   Perspective and Plan, Robie House, Chicago, Illinois
Frank Lloyd Wright 1907
(see Fig. 9.9)

One factor in Wright's changing position was the influence of **Eugene-Emmanuel Viollet-Le-Duc** (1814–79) who stressed the appearance of the building from a normal viewpoint. He also promoted the artistic laws of harmony and balance instead of mere symmetry. This convinced Wright of the need to test his drawings, and the plan in particular, with a perspective of what the building would look like. So he provides these combination drawings of plan and perspective much as Silsbee had done, although scholars of Wright would argue that his motives were completely different. A model for the Robie House and its presentation might have been the Yahara Boat Club in Madison, 1902. From that time the perspective grows in importance. Gradually, the interlocking masses of subsequent prairie houses become more complex until the façade, in a conventional sense, disappears. In the Robie House, the design appears as a woven image of roofs and balconies, shooting past each other in a seemingly unsupported way and providing the kind of visual balance that Viollet-Le-Duc had suggested. It has been shown that Wright returned to many of these principles in the design of Falling Water (Connors 1984).

The famous view of this house was intended. It was set out to achieve the effect following a number of perspective studies from slightly different angles. Wright visited Bear Run Pennsylvania late in 1934, and for nine months thought about designs for the house without putting anything on paper. One morning he received a call from Kaufmann, who said he was just leaving Milwaukee for Taliesin to look at the plans. Wright sat at his drawing board, while two of his students, Edgar Tafel and Bob Moshner, frantically replaced coloured pencils that were used up as fast as they were sharpened. Mesmerized, they watched Wright talking to himself as he laid out the plans for the house. *Lilane and EJ will cross the bridge to walk into the woods . . . The rock on which EJ sits will be the hearth, coming right out of the floor, the fire burning just behind it . . .* His pencil would break and Tafel or Moshner would hand him another. When Kaufmann arrived around lunchtime, the drawings looked as though they had been completed for weeks. The house as it was finally built was almost exactly as Wright had laid it out that morning, with its characteristic dynamic cantilevered reinforced concrete terraces jutting out over the falls (Boulton 1993).

6.3 Sketch Perspective, Falling Water, Bear Run, Pennsylvania
Frank Lloyd Wright with John H Howe
1935
(see Fig. 9.10)

6.4 Sketch Perspective, Guggenheim Museum, New York
Frank Lloyd Wright with John H Howe
1951
(see Figs 5.3, 9.11)

It is sometimes forgotten that Wright was seventy-six years old when he was commissioned to design the Guggenheim Museum, and it was not complete by the time of his death in 1959. The emphasis on the waterfall at Bear Run generates a view in which the house appears in a high, commanding position. In New York, the Guggenheim Museum hovers above the street and is therefore seen at a considerably lower angle. Nevertheless, the principles of composition and balance are clearly evident in the two drawings. All of his perspectives were developed by mechanical projection. The vertical element is to the left in both cases, with a rectilinear plinth stretching out towards the right. The centre of attention is just to the right of the mid point. These perspectives belong to a stylized type of architectural drawing. Unlike realistic scenes, the shapes are positively outlined. Despite the variety of line weight and accents, the buildings are drawn with an almost uniform crispness and an even distribution of emphasis. Relatively strong contrasts occur between the buildings and their settings rather than between the parts of the buildings themselves. Drexler (1962) suggests that much of the pictorial unity of the drawings depends on this regular rendition of architectural forms.

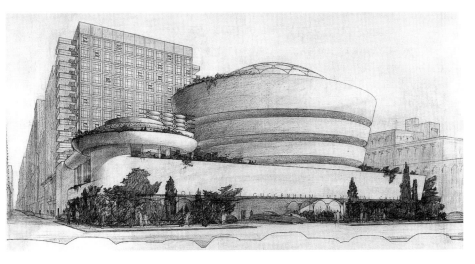

Hugh Ferris (1889–1962) was given the enviable but at the same time unenviable task of producing the images for the proposed United Nations Headquarters in New York. It is difficult to think of a more symbolic project. Between the wars, there had been an attempt at the League of Nations, but the restricted participation meant that it never really became established. At the conclusion of the Second World War, there was another proposal aimed at unifying a number of disparate countries. In that spirit, it was deemed that the designers of the Headquarters should be representative of those nations.

6.5   Sketch of Night View of United Nations Headquarters, New York. Hugh Ferris for Wallace Harrison *et al.* 1947

6.6   Perspective View of the Atheneum (unbuilt) Richard Meier 1979

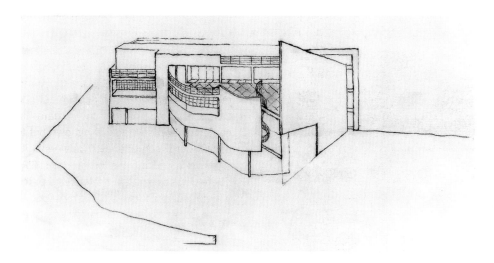

Wallace Harrison chaired a panel of some of the greatest modern architects in the world at that time. They included Le Corbusier, Oscar Niemeyer, Sven Markelius, Howard Robertson and Robert Moses. Daily for eighteen weeks, Ferris worked in harness with the architects, earning their trust as he envisioned their concepts. Each individual was a demanding task master but trying to obtain agreement amongst them needed consummate skill and incredible patience. Fortunately, Hugh Ferris had an uncanny knack of bringing designs to life. In time, all the architects involved, each with his own drawing technique, came to admire this amazing talent. At meeting no. 45, on Monday 9 June 1947, the group needed to resolve which renderings best reflected the architects' ideas, for inclusion in the design report. It had been decided that no other representations of the exterior appearance would be shown in this seminal report. Gradually the architects settled on the four drawings to be presented to the world. As they talked Ferris sat and revised the columns under the General Assembly building, so that Bassov and Le Corbusier could reach agreement over that particular dispute (Dudley 1994).

The consistent, and some would say obsessional, use of modern movement white forms has become the universally recognized signature of **Richard Meier** (b 1934). Clearly influenced by Le Corbusier, he has shown that a gridded geometrical vocabulary is capable of an astonishing variety of expression (Jodidio 1998). For Meier, the search begins with the plan. The two dimensional image contains within it the instructions for the three dimensional object that is the building (Blaser 1996). Yet, like a number of world renowned architects, he expounds the virtues of the design project. The Atheneum, for example, was intended as a centre for visitor orientation and community cultural events. This design is positively Corbusian in terms of forms and their visualization. It is also slightly naïve as the representation of an intended building as the elements appear rather detached from one another. Meier points out that in fact it is no less alive than if it had been completed. His view is that the built and the unbuilt are both imagined three dimensional objects and therefore each enjoys existence on those terms (Meier 1976). It seems that his real desire is to express clarity of form and that is at the heart of his ongoing investigation.

6.7 Perspective of the Barcelona Museum of Contemporary Art
Richard Meier 1987

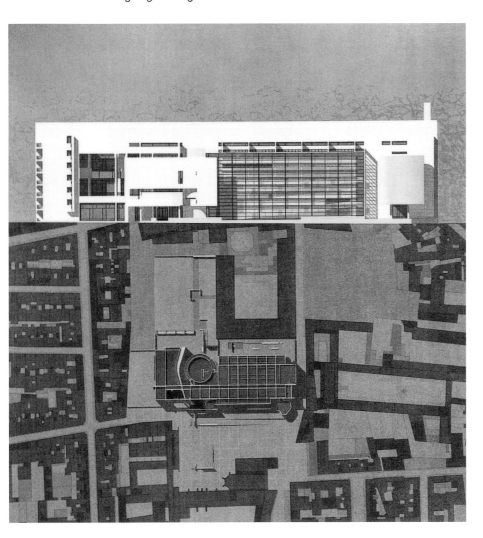

Not surprisingly, the grid appears in every aspect of the Barcelona Museum of Contemporary Art, capturing the richness between past and present. Meier presents a perspective view on top of the street plan, as if he is trying to emphasize that the architecture is a visual continuity of the exterior patterns (Meier 1997). It is such a flat view that the perspective almost appears in elevation. Again, there is a kind of resonance with an aerial view of the district which is almost like a plan but retains converging lines in the height of the buildings. Dollens observes that the museum itself moves in and out of focus according to the visitor's stride. Consequently, static geometric forms are shifted in a continuous play of light and shadow (Meier 1997). This is noticeably more crisp and precise as a depiction and design than the Atheneum. Meier has moved on from the influence of Le Corbusier, not only to create a contemporary language of his own but to display a consistency between its representation and the finished building. There is a superb balance in the asymmetric façade and an immense sophistication that has been a significant development from his earlier work.

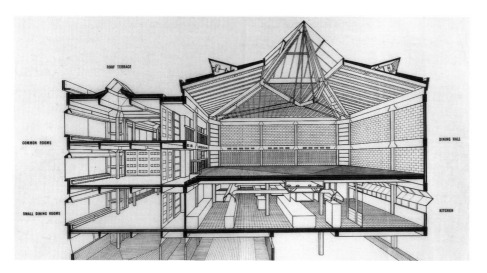

ROOF TERRACE

COMMON ROOMS

DINING HALL

SMALL DINING ROOMS

KITCHEN

6.8　Sectional Perspective, University Centre, Cambridge
Howell Killick Partridge and Amis 1963
(see Fig. 5.11)

This sectional perspective by **HKPA** is quite a hard edged drawing. It shows the complexity of the structure over the Dining Hall, and patterns on the walls and floors. There is a hint that the large volume is flanked by a group of smaller volumes. These are articulated by what Pevsner calls the motifs of the moment in fashion – excessive canting and chamfering (Booth and Taylor 1970). The drawing is one of a series that describes the form and spaces in some detail (HKPA 1981) while never really offering what the atmosphere of the building might be like.

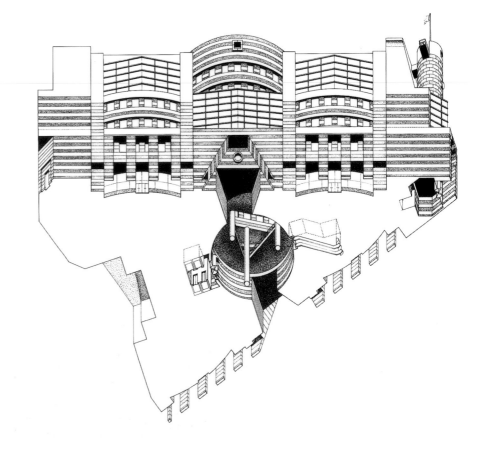

6.9　Up-view Axonometric, No. 1 Poultry, London
James Stirling Michael Wilford and Associates 1986
(see Figs 5.16, 10.23)

According to **Michael Wilford**, when a single concept has been agreed with a client, the practice develops a full range of up and down view axonometrics, isometrics, perspectives etc. Wilford feels that the actual viewpoint from which the building is drawn is critically important and can often only be determined after experimentation. He also contends that the design drawings convey, to the practised eye, a correct and factual architectural understanding of the building and not confused or subjective *Artists' Impressions*. The practice uses axonometrics a great deal and Wilford admits that they are preferred because the spaces, surfaces and volumetrics of a design can be set out in a single image (Wilford, Muirhead, Maxwell 1994). His claim that there is no distortion or guesswork involved in an accurate reading of the building is less convincing. Wilford's case that the vertical and horizontal planes are drawn at the same scale, and that the axo can be very useful in explaining the more complex parts of the project, is fair enough. Yet, the mechanical appearance of axonometrics can misrepresent the final building appearance as there is always emphasis on roof or floor.

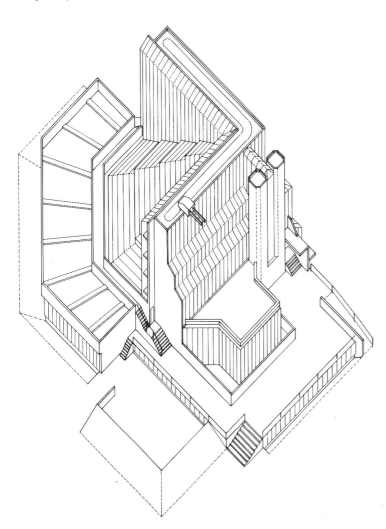

6.10 Axonometric, History Faculty Library, Cambridge University
James Stirling 1964

Moreover the distortion to the rear corner caused by lack of perspective can actually give a distorted impression. In a critique of **James Stirling**'s History Faculty Library, Booth and Taylor (1970) argue that with a building conceived and drawn as a section and an axonometric that can only be seen from a helicopter, it is disturbing to have to look at a flat-on elevation. They point out that the lift and stair towers are in fact much less slim than they looked on the drawing. In addition, the glass walling turns out to be much stiffer than its representation and the diagonals featured in the design are not visible from various angles. This does not really accord with Stirling's statement that the completed building is almost identical to the original design. John Jacobus considers that the building appears to be a continuation of the style of Leicester and it has been difficult to see the Cambridge design except in relation to the earlier work. He continues that with Stirling's characteristic axonometric type of drawing, the family resemblance is inescapable (Stirling 1975). There is more than a hint that these are built paper patterns.

Norman Foster (b. 1935) makes a number of points about the design stages of a building project, which are epitomized by the Sainsbury Centre. He writes that it would be easy to take for granted by the architects but may not be so obvious to the reader. The design evolution of a project is rarely a simple linear route, the actual process being far more circuitous than might be imagined from the outside. He reflects on the way that the tools have since become more sophisticated but the process of design is as pragmatic as ever. The computer, like the pencil, is only as good as the person directing it (Foster *et al.* 1989). There are numerous drawings (and models) of this project at various stages of design development. Some explore the junctions between the various components but most are three dimensional explanations of the form and the way that components slot into that form. The medium chosen most often was isometric projection. There is something about the directional form of this design that lends itself to isometric representation. As a three dimensional slice through the building, it almost illustrates the entire message, from component to concept.

6.11 Sectional Isometric, Sainsbury Centre, UEA, Norwich
Foster Associates c. 1975

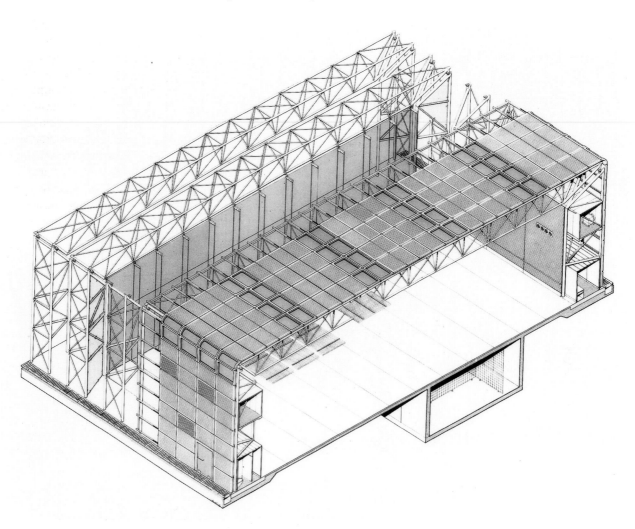

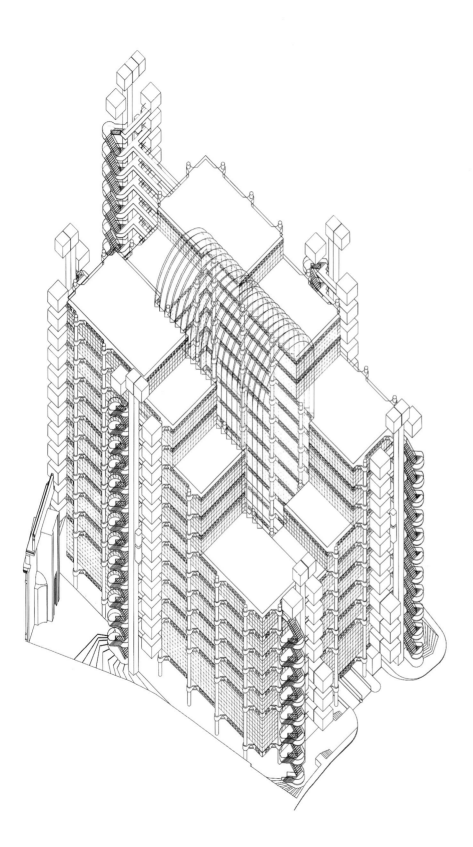

It takes some studying but it is possible to see the imagery of a medieval castle in the design of the Lloyds building by the **Richard Rogers Partnership**. The trick is to ignore the materials and look at the form. It is just one of many contradictions in a building which could equally well demonstrate an evolutionary design process or a revolutionary design theme that started with Archigram and was the essence of the Centre Georges Pompidou. Services are pushed to the periphery to open-up usable areas at the core. The main purpose of the axonometric is to illustrate this underlying principle of a form that is generated by working spaces ringed by a series of service towers (Powell 1999). The direction from the South West is well chosen, as it shows the progressive stepping up of the form around the atrium, almost reminiscent of an Escher staircase. Both the Sainsbury Centre and the Lloyds Building are pieces of engineering as much as they are buildings. The drawings also have similar characteristics. They come from that immediate pre-CAD period in which sharp, precise ruled pen lines delineated forms and components alike.

6.12 Axonometric from South West, Lloyds of London.
Richard Rogers Partnership c. 1980
(see Figs 5.15, 9.24)

The objective of this drawing is to show two office blocks that match the size of others on London Wall but achieve a more human scale at ground level. In the description of the scheme, much emphasis is placed on cut-away axonometrics at ground and first floor levels, showing dense and welcoming pedestrian spaces (Moore, 1987). Nevertheless, the illustrated view is the most frequently displayed drawing of this project and the one that epitomizes the building design. There is a kind of pride in size that is being expressed. This seems to be emphasized by the concept of two similar blocks set at an angle to one another. If it were just one block, it would appear as a single monument and the impact of the drawing would be quite different. The layout also disguises the axonometric projection. Neither of the blocks is set at the traditional 45°. This produces a number of visual effects. There is a feeling of movement generated, as if the forms were just settling into position. The distortion at the rear corner, normally associated with this type of projection, is greatly reduced. Further amelioration of that problem is achieved by the barrel vaulted roof.

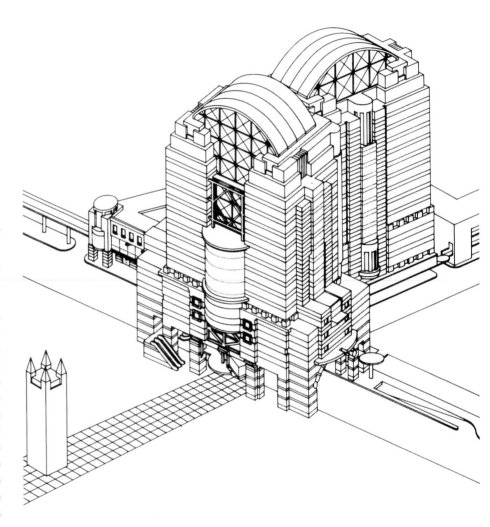

6.13   Axonometric, Lee House, Alban Gate, London
Terry Farrell and Partners 1987
(see Figs 5.17, 8.19)

6.14 Perspective, Charing Cross, Embankment Place, London

Terry Farrell and Partners 1987

(see Figs 5.19, 9.27)

The power and scale of the building design are clearly evident in this representation. There is also a suggestion of the way that the building is slotted into an urban space at the heart of London, with the existing volumes shown in block form. As expected from **Terry Farrell and Partners**, the development of Embankment Place involved the preparation of thousands of sketches, presentation, working and detail drawings (Binney 1991). There is a strong notion of enjoyment in the illustration of the scheme, as if all the architects involved, wished to make a contribution to the understanding of how the completed building will look. The fact that there is little consistency in the style of the representations somehow does not seem to matter. There is always concern among architects about the coherence of project presentations. With this architectural practice, it is possible to see a number of styles in the drawings, running between the projects while each scheme has a variety. It is almost as if the design is being tested by different individuals, each coming from a different viewpoint and each with his or her own means of expression.

6.15   Freehand Perspective, Aqua Vale Swimming Centre, Aylesbury, Buckinghamshire
FaulknerBrowns 1998

The purpose of this drawing was to illustrate the impact of the proposed building on the park in which it was to be set. It is a sensitive area for a large building and the perspective helped to re-assure both local authority planning officers and local residents. According to **FaulknerBrowns** the benefit of producing a freehand drawing is mainly related to timescale. They point out that CAD modelling needs to be convincing and detail of that kind takes longer to develop. They do not favour the block CAD models but recognize that thoroughly conceived computer generated images are powerful tools. By contrast, hand drawings are perceived as cartoons that can be projected onto a screen at large scale during client presentations. The interiors show how the building might come alive. One combination of techniques often used is a model to show the exterior and drawings to show the interior. However, in the case of Aqua Vale Swimming Centre, people could not visualize the scale of the building from the model. Neither the exterior nor the interior perspective is produced by mechanical construction. Mostly, they are three dimensional representations of plans and sections.

Even the Corus interior began as a section from which the one point perspective was created. The medium is surprisingly low-tech. This drawing was originally produced on butter paper with a fine liner pen. It is all part of the practice's philosophy of telling a design story, in which all the models and drawings are aimed at illustrating particular aspects of the design. They do not favour one *Artist's Impression* that stands out from the rest of the presentation, and in some way is supposed to summarize the scheme. The objective is to show the design work rather than produce a set of architects' drawings plus one specific illustration. Therefore the practice tries to undertake all the presentations in-house, as if they were presenting their own design service of a spirit that is in the concept and a style that is in the architecture. Telling the story of the design involves a similar language in all the drawings, so that they appear as a cohesive group. At the same time the images can be perceived at different levels, so that professionals and members of the public can all derive impressions from them. This is a particularly useful feature where competition entries are concerned.

6.16   Interior Perspective, Corus Research, Development and Technology Centre, Sheffield
FaulknerBrowns 2000

From the outside, FaulknerBrowns are viewed as the epitome of a corporate practice. The perception is of a systems-driven organization in which employees become part of the machine. The reputation for management efficiency and high-tech buildings adds to this perception. It is generally assumed, therefore, that drawings are part of a production process that employs the latest electronic equipment. While this undoubtedly does occur, it is interesting to discover the level of individuality that still remains in the design process. It may be that illustration methods become expedient due to time pressures and it may be that competitions and actual commissions are treated differently. Yet, there is something enriching about the way that both Terry Farrell and Partners and FaulknerBrowns demonstrate a variety of presentation methods – compared with practices that insist on a shared discipline of drawing. The difference between these two practices is that the former shows the variety within each project while the latter shows it between projects.

6.17   Perspective View from Castle, Competition for Inland Revenue Offices, Nottingham
Michael Hopkins and Partners 1992

The **Michael Hopkins and Partners** winning entry combines metal and masonry in the manner of 19th century industrial buildings. Commentators have described it in a variety of ways. To some its round staircase towers are romantic and castle-like. To others, the presentation evokes the functional tradition that shaped the Victorian fringes of Nottingham and attempts to reconnect this now isolated site with the pattern of the city centre. **Arup Associates** show the galleria and garden as seen from Nottingham Castle (AJ 26 February 1992), with a large planted court between the proposed and existing.

An over-riding modernist ethos that tends to exclude any other type of contribution was stridently expressed in the commentaries of this competition result. It may also have been in the minds of the judges. Certainly, the people of Nottingham did not see it that way. Their votes did not favour either of these two schemes. On the face of it, higher quality design should come out of a competitive situation. However, the same names seem to recur with great regularity. The question is whether these practices are really significantly better than all the others in Britain or whether the competition system promotes favourites amongst the metropolitan elite. This is an interesting opportunity to directly compare two similar drawings. The Arup Associates' version is slightly more detailed in terms of context but actually would have been a more convincing proposal without the foreground. At first sight the Hopkins' competition entry does seem to respond to the existing turreted building in the foreground. The cylinders with lids are situated at either side of the entrance way. Yet, the notion of a special design for Nottingham loses some credibility when other work by this practice is studied.

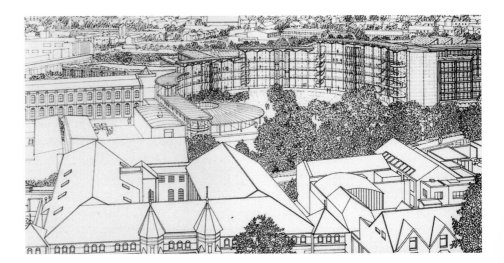

6.18   Perspective View from Castle, Competition for Inland Revenue Offices, Nottingham
Arup Associates 1992

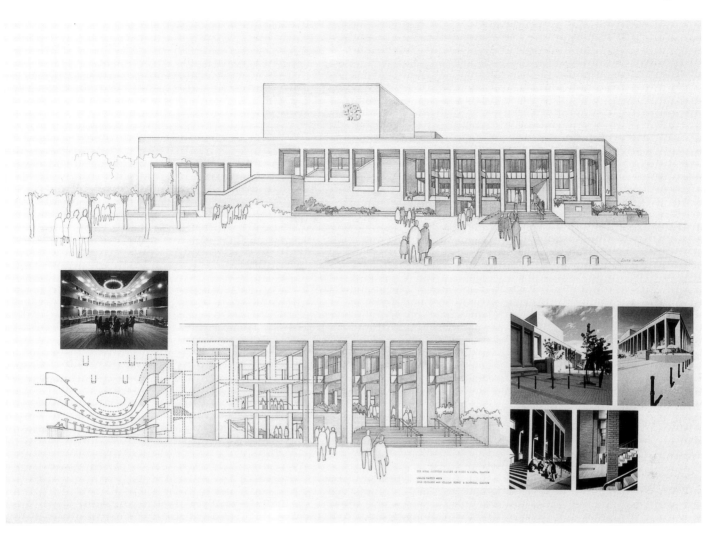

6.19 **Perspective Views, Scottish Academy, Glasgow**
Leslie Martin 1982

The initial concept for this project was taken to a fully developed scheme stage in the Cambridge studio of **Leslie Martin** (1908–2000). From this stage, the executive architects, William Nimmo and Partners of Glasgow, were responsible for developing the detailed design and production drawings. It should always be the case that design drawings explain the full intentions but where a project is handed on to others, it becomes a real necessity. In *Background and Belief*, Martin uses the word *compose* to describe the central activity of an architect. The apparent simple composition of this design belies the complexity of the many, often conflicting requirements (AJ 11 May 1988). Illustrated is a set presented to the RIBA Drawings Collection. It shows small inset photographs of the completed interior and exterior of the building alongside Martin's original perspective of the main frontage. The other view shows the free standing pier system. The depth and recession are increased by the way in which the structural lines are carried through into the building itself (Martin 1983). The clarity of the concept is exemplified by this attractive and deceptively simple drawing style.

Around the early to middle part of the 20th century, a special period occurred. Britain had been slow to embrace modernism and European architects were leading the way. For various reasons, not least the growing Nazi threat, a number of these architects started to work in Britain. Others, such as Le Corbusier and Mies van der Rohe, were influential through the work that they were completing, principally in France and the United States of America. During this period, the drawings continued to be both two dimensional and three dimensional but the style had changed to match the architecture. Detail and decoration were virtually forbidden. The external material was invariably concrete or stucco which presented plain surfaces that were just drawn in outline. The design process seemed more analytical. Circulation patterns for different users were sometimes shown on the plans to explain from where the layout had been derived. Houses and education buildings appeared to receive the most attention but the style of presentation and design methods employed were applicable to any building type.

7.0   Perspective of Sunspan House
Wells Coates 1934

Contemporary journals had been reporting that for some time continental designers were devoting their attention to the application of concrete to the problem of the smaller house. A definite technique was evolving but doubts were being expressed as to whether the box-like appearance with flat roof is suitable for British taste and climate (AR October 1926). Completed in 1925, New Ways was the first private house in the international style to be built in England. It was advertised as an opportunity to see a house of this character although not built of concrete. The owner, Mr WJ Basset-Lowke, felt that considerable interest would be aroused by the arrival of this challenging and spirited stranger, designed by Prof. Dr. **Peter Behrens** (1868–1940) of Vienna. It even had to incorporate a room from an earlier house by Charles Rennie Mackintosh (Windsor 1981). The plans are drawn in a precise, mechanical and conventional manner, indicating a reproduction. However, the drawing for the hall floor, laid out with large and small tiles in black, white and grey, is in shaded freehand and clearly a design drawing by Behrens. Yet it is the representation of the exterior form that grabs most attention.

7.1   Perspective of New Ways, Wellingborough Road Northampton
Peter Behrens 1923

The theme of *Thin Straight Lines* is more figurative than totally literal. Some of the drawings do not have thin lines and some of the forms are actually curved. Nevertheless, there was a period in the first half of the 20th century when both drawings and buildings appeared as outlines of planar surfaces, generally intended to be concrete. They were mostly devoid of detail and often appeared brash and stark. The association of drawing and design has probably never been closer than during this period of the modern movement and its international style.

In modernist architecture, the years up to 1932 mark the summit of German achievement. Except for Behrens, progressive architects who remained in Germany after that date did little or no work. **Erich Mendelsohn** (1887–1953) left to avoid persecution and in summer 1933 came to England. Charles Reilly, Professor of Architecture at Liverpool University, was delighted. He wrote in *Scaffolding the Sky* (London 1938) that Mendelsohn is *the most brilliant architect in Europe of the modern school*. However, England had its limitations. FRS Yorke noted in the first edition of his international survey *The Modern House* (London 1937) that the 14 pages devoted to England had been difficult to fill. Modernist designs were frequently opposed and either refused planning permission or granted permission only with the proviso that compromises were made. Such circumstances may partly account for the fact that during his six years in England, Mendelsohn would build very little (Stephan 1999). Yet having won an architectural competition in 1934, with Serge Chermayaff (1900–96), he was at least able to produce one major public building (Zevi 1999). The municipal social centre at Bexhill comprises the Popular De La Warr Pavilion and a swimming pool.

Unusually, the brief, which attracted 200 entries, was for a modern design (Whittick 1956). Mendelsohn's idiosyncratic sketches convey the form and status of the intended building in very few lines. He was a born expressionist. The images emerge free from constraints, and invariably the lack of context goes unnoticed as he shows an almost endless comparison between vision and architecture. Nearly always, the skyward push towards infinity is restrained by a metaphysical arch. Zevi (1999) suggests that one of the most reliable ways of becoming an architect is to analyse these sketches. They pick out horizontal and vertical elements that are the essence of his designs and the epitome of modernism. Illustrated is an early variant of the scheme, with a multi-storey hotel on the South West corner of the site and a cinema to the North East. They were abandoned, probably for reasons of cost (Stephan 1999). The pavilion can be seen in the centre as a series of horizontal decks with the characteristic semi-circular glazed staircase tower. These became symbolic of Mendelsohn's architecture, and his way of introducing dynamism and excitement into a number of projects that were otherwise simple rectilinear forms.

7.2   Perspective Sketch of De La Warr Pavilion, Bexhill on Sea, Sussex
Eric Mendelsohn 1934

Marcel Breuer (1902–81) was the Hungarian-born Director of the Furniture Workshop at the Bauhaus, 1925–28. He moved to England in 1934 and designed furniture for a firm called Isokon while in practice with **FRS Yorke** (1906–62), before moving to the USA in 1937. FRS had been a founder member of the MARS Group since 1933, and later established the well-known architectural practice Yorke, Rosenberg and Mardall. Yorke and Breuer were dedicated to modern domestic building and used the thin straight line technique without a hint of the materials or construction.

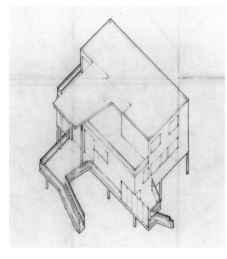

7.3 Axonometric of House at Angmerling on Sea, Sussex
FRS Yorke and Marcel Breuer 1936

7.4 Plans, Sections and Elevations of House at Milvil Road, Lee-on-Solent, Hampshire
FRS Yorke and Marcel Breuer 1936

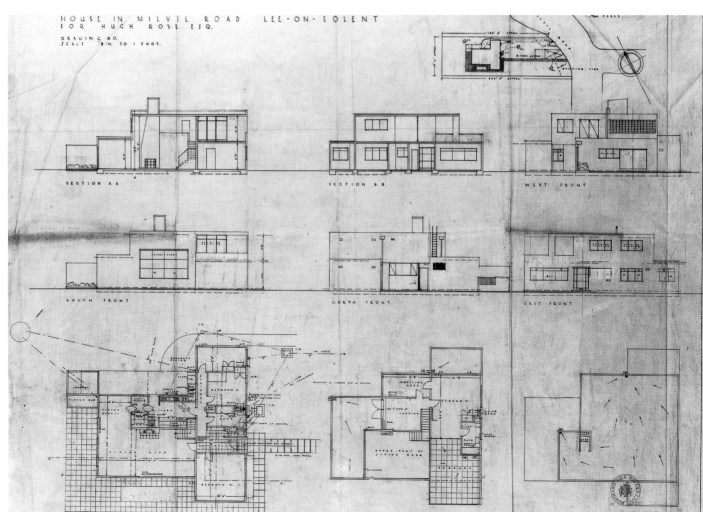

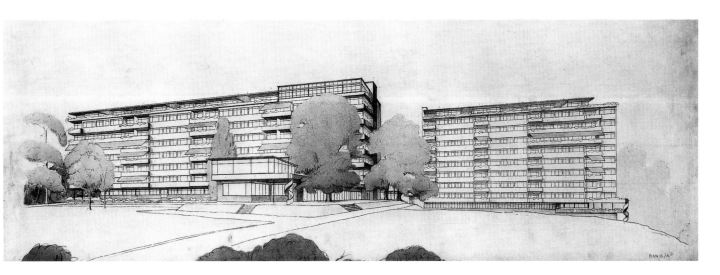

7.5 Perspective of Flats at St Leonard's Hill, Windsor, Berkshire, for Isokon Ltd
Walter Gropius 1935

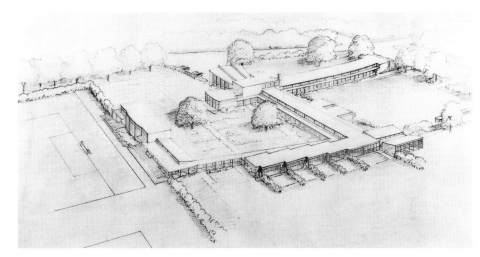

7.6 Aerial Perspective of Impington Village College, Cambridgeshire
Walter Gropius and Maxwell Fry 1936

The founder of the famous Bauhaus at Weimar in 1919 was the German **Walter Gropius** (1883–1969). He came to England in 1934, to work with **E Maxwell Fry** (1899–1987) on a block of flats in Manchester for Isokon. The two were briefly partners from 1936 to 1937 before Gropius moved to the USA as Professor of Architecture at Harvard. Isokon had plans for a number of building projects but nearly all of them went unfulfilled. Gropius came close with his proposal at St Leonard's Hill (Peto and Loveday 1999) for two blocks of 110 apartments (Gropius, I. 1972).

However, their connections with Isokon enabled Gropius and Fry to be introduced to Henry Morris, Director of Education for Cambridgeshire. His schemes for rural education were already established but sought their expression in contemporary architecture. Fry notes that the college they designed for the parkland by the village of Impington set a standard that animated all school building to follow (Fry 1975). It was a new idea to use a school also as a community centre and everything about it was perceived as modern. The elevated viewpoint of the drawing highlights the expanse of flat roof. There are dynamic shapes, as in the main hall, and a curve in the eastern corridor that does not seem to have any purpose. It is actually difficult to see how form follows function in this case. It is probably due to the influence of Gropius that the aerial view is in perspective, rather than isometric, and that the implied courtyards are as much defined by planting as the building. Fry was another founder member of the MARS (Modern Architecture Research) Group and according to Stephen Bayley, the only native Englishman to play a full part in the establishment of modern architecture in England (AD November 1979).

FLATS   AT   LAWN   ROAD   WELLS   COATES   ARCHITECT

In December 1931, a furniture manufacturer named Jack Pritchard (1899–1992) had established Isokon, based on *Isometric Unit construction*. It was intended that the company should make houses, flats, furniture and fittings in units and these were to be designed by Pritchard's friend, **Wells Coates** (1895–1958), who apparently was fond of using isometric drawings (Peto and Loveday 1999). Coates had been born in Japan to Canadian parents and had studied engineering in Vancouver and London. He was an ebullient character whose arguable lack of originality was overshadowed by his enthusiasm and diligence. He was also a founder member of MARS and a member of the Twentieth Century Group. While Isokon involved some of the best designers in Europe to produce a significant output of furniture, its only memorial in terms of building is the Lawn Road Flats. Few developments can boast such a distinguished list of tenants. This one-time show piece of the Modern Movement in Britain once provided homes for Walter Gropius, Marcel Breuer, Moholy-Nagy and Agatha Christie and gave temporary accommodation to Siegried Giedion and Le Corbusier, amongst others (AD 10 November 1979).

7.7   Perspective of Flats at Lawn Road, London
Wells Coates 1932

The depiction of the flats in perspective is interesting. It might have been expected that such a rectilinear form would have been shown in isometric. The stark white appearance is emphasized by the dark shading of the sky. The angle of the drawing and this contrast of light and dark are a little reminiscent of Mackintosh's technique for presentations (see Fig. 4.21). The view was also well chosen to show the cantilevered external balconies and the main staircase at the northern end as a vertical element to terminate the horizontal lines. The finished building has been frequently photographed from a similar angle. The concept of *minimum dwelling* on which the Lawn Road Flats were based, evolved out of Le Corbusier, through Maxwell Fry and the Exhibition of British Industrial Art at Dorland Hall. According to Wells, nearly all the credit for the ideas behind the building was given to Molly Pritchard. Nevertheless, it is Coates' Lawn Road Flats that appeared as an ideogram for a whole generation of English architects (Cantacuzino 1978) and its perspective drawing is one of the enduring images of 1930s modern architecture in Britain, as a number of architects have returned to both the drawing and the building.

Berthold Lubetkin (1901–90) was born in Georgia and moved to England in 1930. **Tecton** was formed around him in 1932. Lubetkin was aware of the lack of theoretical background among his partners and used the architectural projects to evolve a method for the analysis of the requirements, meticulously recording it as part of the process and reasoning behind the designs. The proposed Chest Clinic at East Ham was used as a teaching vehicle within the practice. The external form has been called ungainly, due to the schematic nature of the design. The problems of circulation and location of functions were dissected in a series of cumulative overlays depicting combinations of route and use throughout the building. However, it remained a paper project which brought no immediate commissions and Lubetkin nearly returned to Russia. The practice was saved by a commission to design the Gorilla House for London Zoo in late 1932. In this project, the Tecton partners continued to develop their research techniques as an integral part of the design. They felt that only through a process of separating the factual from the speculative could any genuine solution be appropriately synthesized. In the sequence of five drawings, the scheme evolves

through general planning considerations to air-current and insulation diagrams, which tested the reliability of the working thesis. The Chest Clinic and Gorilla House drawings represent a rational but radical procedure towards a valid modern architecture. The care in the preparation of these drawings and their use as publicity material disclose a wider intention than that of making sophisticated office records of the group's development of a design. Lubetkin later pointed out that the absence of agreed aims and principles inhibited proper understanding of contemporary architecture (AR March 1951). The widespread publication of Tecton drawings disseminated evidence. The quality of the analysis enabled them to pre-empt the viewer's next question by explaining a particular solution in relation to the developing programme. Thus the designs became accessible as the drawings are readily understandable by all. They were invariably the work of **Lindsay Drake** (1909–80) whose enthusiasm and graphic skill communicated the Tecton message. With Lubetkin's advice, Drake completed the early drawings, to be joined in later work by the expertise of staff such as William Tatton-Brown and Gordon Cullen (Coe and Reading 1981).

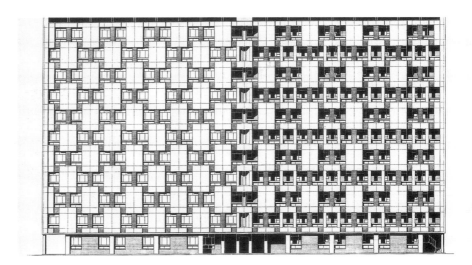

7.8   Elevation of Dorset Estate, Bethnal Green, London
Berthold Lubetkin and Tecton 1934

7.9   Perspective of Chest Clinic, East Ham, London
Berthold Lubetkin and Tecton 1932

7.10   Plan and Circulation Patterns, Chest Clinic, East Ham, London
Berthold Lubetkin and Tecton 1932

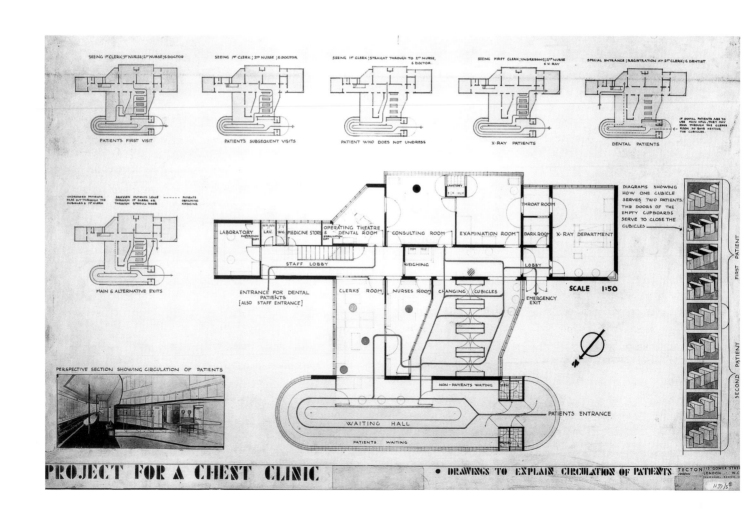

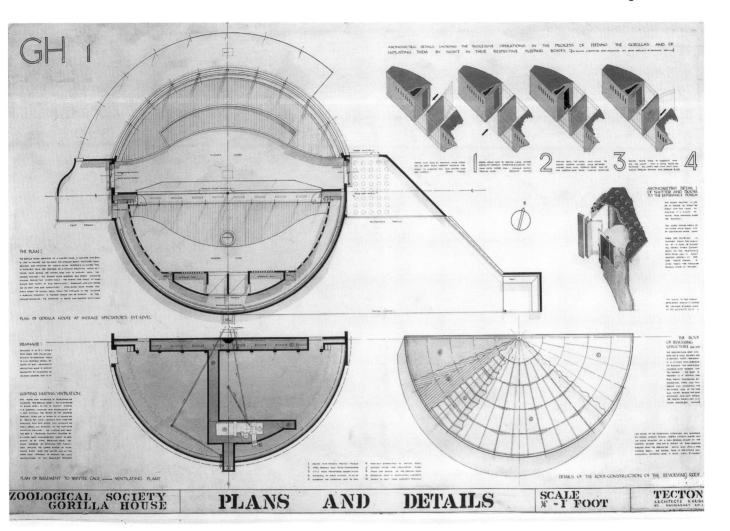

7.11 Plans and Details, Gorilla House, Zoological Society, London
Berthold Lubetkin and Tecton 1932

The analytical form of Tecton's design presentations was part of a continuous attempt to establish modern architecture in Britain on a sounder intellectual footing. Lubetkin felt that it could be achieved through the MARS Group and the Tecton office all joined. However, his interest soon dissipated as it became increasingly obvious that the Group was not interested in a systematic programme of research. MARS Group members were essentially absorbed in stylistic preferences and aesthetic dogma. Tecton went much further. They analysed the design process into appropriate strategies which meant that the solutions could be tested. Then, importantly, they showed how the parts could be synthesized into an evolving building. Often partners in architectural practices work on specific projects for their own clients. Sometimes this leads to a lack of coherence in the output and the subjectivity associated with individual enterprise. Bethnal Green, the Chest Clinic and the Gorilla House are clearly a group effort, objective and thoroughly consistent. The work is punctuated with spirited maxims, including that it is *better to spend a month drawing than spoil the building for ever* (Coe and Reading 1981).

British modern architecture may not have existed as a force at all, had it not been for the East European emigrés. Behrens was a visitor but Mendelsohn, Breuer, Lubetkin and **Erno Goldfinger** (1902–87) all came to live in England during the early 1930s. Although born in Budapest, Goldfinger had been secretary of the French delegation to the Congrès International d'Architecture Moderne in 1933. He was keen to join the MARS Group on his arrival in London. However, he became disenchanted with it for similar reasons to Lubetkin. Goldfinger felt that the allusions to research and social purpose were more pretension than reality. In 1937, he seized the opportunity to design three houses in Willow Road opposite Hampstead Heath, of which the middle house was to be his own. The drawing is interesting in that it emphasizes a matter of principle. The walls appear solid and show that the intended material is brickwork. It therefore verged on the ridiculous when local opposition accused Erno of proposing a Corbusian white box. The argument that he had really designed a modern interpretation of the traditional terrace overwhelmingly won the day (Dunnet and Stamp 1983).

7.12   Perspective of 1–3 Willow Road, Hampstead, London
Erno Goldfinger 1937

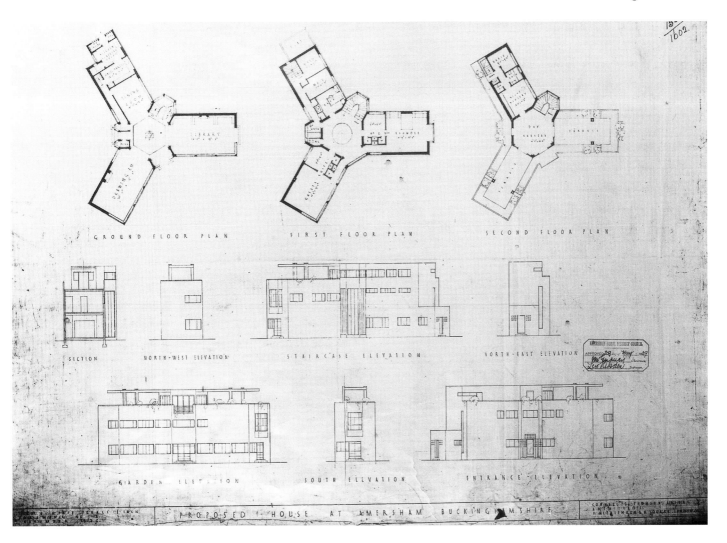

7.13 **Plans and Elevations of 'High and Over' House at Amersham, Buckinghamshire**
Amyas Connell 1929

Amyas Connell (1901–80) had just graduated from the British School at Rome when he received his first commission. 'High and Over' became the boldest modern building to appear in Britain in the 1920s. Connell had a great admiration for classicism but this house stands as a landmark in the development of modern architecture. In 1931, he formed a well-known partnership with **Basil Ward** (1902–76) and **Colin Lucas** (1906–94). They worked on other modern houses such as Melchet Court but by 1939, the partnership had been dissolved.

7.14 **Axonometric of House at Melchet Court, Wiltshire**
Connell, Ward and Lucas 1937

It hardly needs to be stated that the central figure in modernist architecture was Charles-Edouard Jeanneret, better known as **Le Corbusier** (1887–1965). His fascination with axonometric projection has been well recorded and he has been identified as one of the first to perceive axonometry as the *homogeneous and transparent space of modernity* (Monnier 1985). Yet an examination of his sketchbooks from 1914 to 1964 reveals how he consistently used perspective views to visualize his ideas. There is not a single axonometric as an initial idea for a building. The majority of his iconic axonometrics are found in the late 1920s and early 1930s, including this bird's-eye view of the Villa Savoye. After 1935, axonometry appears rarely and by the 1960s, he seems to have abandoned three dimensional representation altogether as his drawings take on a flat collage-like quality (Perez-Gomez and Pelletier 1997). Villa Savoye is the epitome of the white box, so feared by the British establishment. Much has been made of Le Corbusier as an avant-garde post-cubist painter but it is not evident in the presentation of this pure design. In fact, the drawing is hard, straight edged and mechanical.

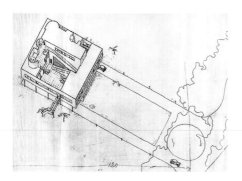

7.15 Axonometric of Villa Savoye, Poissy

Le Corbusier 1929

(see Fig. 9.12)

7.16 Perspective of Maisons Jaoul, Neuilly sur Seine

Le Corbusier 1951

(see Fig. 9.14)

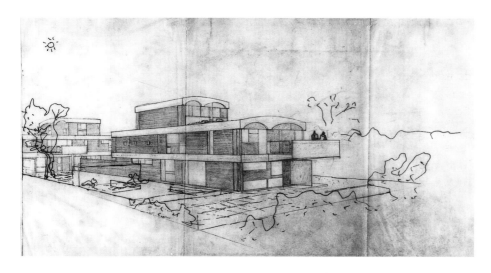

There is a slightly disturbing notion about identical houses designed for father and son, on the same site (Lyon 2000). The Jaoul Houses were conceived twenty two years after the Villa Savoye and despite some of the forms, there is something of a return to traditionalism in both the design and its depiction. They are instantly recognisable as houses, set in gardens off a street. There are front doors, walls and windows. The envelope separates outside from inside and there are no terraces or roof gardens. In terms of the drawing, there is less of an abstract quality. The buildings appear solid and brickwork is discernible as the walling material. It is a raised perspective rather than bird's-eye axonometric and although the perspective has become a little elongated, there is a comprehensible realism about the proposal. The twin houses were among his last private residences. From this time onwards, Le Corbusier began to concentrate on mass housing and other large developments. It is fascinating how this project appears to disturb modernist commentators. Some just choose to ignore it. Admittedly, the roughness of the product is not apparent in the drawing and perhaps the reality is rather coarse. Moreover, there are some inconsistent shapes and strange projections from parts of the buildings that do not assist the artistic effect. Yet, as a drawing, it has much to offer. Although the view is raised, there is a human scale and definition in the external spaces. Closer inspection of the buildings themselves generates doubts about the assertion that they were intended to be identical houses. The windows are on different elevations and the forms are not exactly replicated. It seems more likely that Le Corbusier was experimenting with a geometry that appears consistent while actually offering a number of significant variations between the two dwellings.

If there was discomfort with the Jaoul Houses, there was nothing but praise for the Pilgrimage Chapel at Ronchamp. Arguably Le Corbusier's most successful building, at last the promise of concrete as a plastic material was realized. A built piece of sculpture with which everybody can relate, it seems to be a gem beyond criticism. The drawing is one of the few axonometrics to appear in his mature work. Maybe it was the only way that he could include all of its features together. In *Towards A New Architecture* he wrote that *the Plan is the generator* (Le Corbusier 1923). Thus, he needed to show this plan precisely. He could also demonstrate the relationship between the interior and the external altar. Yet, it is the third dimension that completes the composition. The interior drama is heightened by the shafts of white and coloured light. In this depiction, Le Corbusier is able to set out the sizes, shapes and positions of the apertures punched through the thick walls. The drawing is completed by the tower, which responds to the curves of the plan. This is still a mechanical drawing but it describes the building so well, as a complete entity.

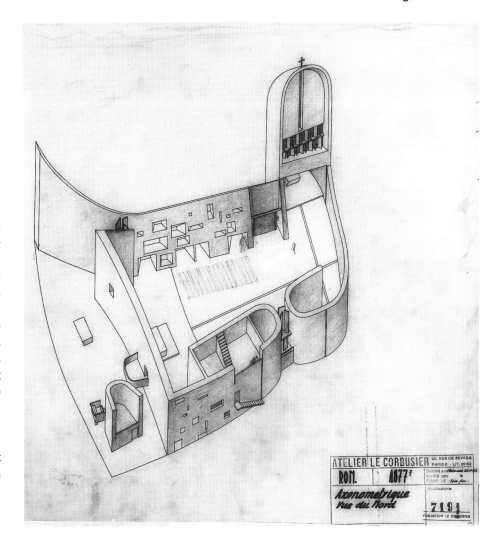

7.17 Axonometric of Chapelle Notre Dame du Haut Ronchamp
Le Corbusier 1950
(see Fig. 9.15)

It is difficult to say whether the young Jeanneret was fortunate in the people he met or whether he had an intent to seek them out. From Art School at La Chaux-de-Fonds, Corbu went to work for Auguste Perret, a classicist who was becoming a pioneer in the development of reinforced concrete framed buildings. This was the second step on his journey. The dream of many young designers at that time was to work with Peter Behrens. Corbu managed to obtain a special fellowship from his former Art School and realized his dream. It is quite remarkable that while in Behren's studio, he worked with two fellow apprentices named Walter Gropius and Ludwig Mies van der Rohe. It was the alliance of Gropius, Mies and Le Corbusier, under Behrens' tutorship, that sowed the seeds for the entire development of modern architecture. They were all artists and despite their interests in the workings of machinery, it was the emergence of a new aesthetic language that captured their imaginations. They aspired to pure geometry, precision, a machine art. However, the suggestion is that, surprisingly, none of them ever generated a consistent means of showing this graphically in their designs (Blake 1960).

Ludwig Mies van der Rohe (1886–1969) is renowned for the most precise buildings. The Farnsworth House, Seagram Building and the Apartment Buildings at Lake Shore Drive are all in that most exacting form of modern architecture – expressed geometrical frame with glass infill. It might have been expected, therefore, that his design drawings would be very descriptive; showing the exact proposals from concept to detail. They actually appear quite vague, and as the essence of the thin straight line technique. Only with the Farnsworth House elevation is there the slightest indication of context. In *Artists' Pictures* (Chapter 4), it was demonstrated how design drawings almost became an end in themselves. With Mies, it was all about the product (Blaser 1981). There are numerous photographs of the finished buildings and they are a delight. Several schemes have also been drawn as post-construction illustrations (Carter 1974). Nevertheless, without solid original drawings, there remains an intangible elusiveness about the design phase. Even Drexler (1960) who provided wonderful insight to Frank Lloyd Wright's drawings, focuses on the completed buildings of Mies van der Rohe.

7.18 Preliminary North Elevation, Farnsworth House, Fox River, Plano, Illinois
Ludwig Mies van der Rohe 1946

7.19 Partial Elevation, Seagram Building, New York
Ludwig Mies van der Rohe 1954

7.20 Exterior Perspective, Apartment Buildings, 860/880 Lake Shore Drive, Chicago, Illinois
Ludwig Mies van der Rohe 1948

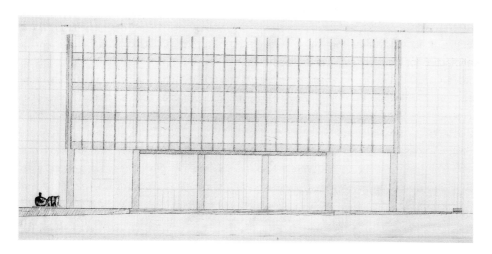

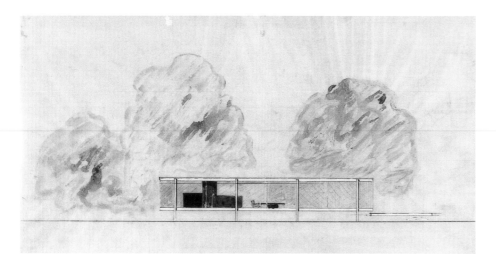

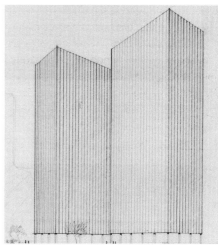

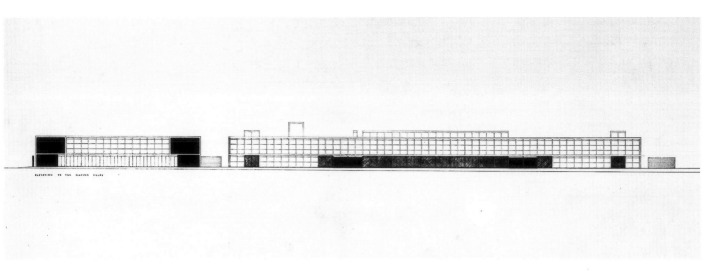

7.21 Elevations of Hunstanton School, Norfolk.
Alison and Peter Smithson 1950

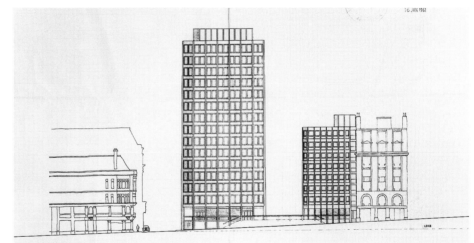

7.22 Bury Street Elevation, the Economist Building, London.
Alison and Peter Smithson 1961

Alison (1928–1993) and **Peter Smithson** (b 1923) were the foremost British disciples of Mies van der Rohe. The evidence is at Hunstanton. The gridded elevations appear long, low and flat. In fact they are very similar to the working drawings. The School represented the start of a period that the architects termed *The Shift* which relates to a change in the aesthetics of their architecture. They perceived an inventive energy that was beginning to stir in England. It reached its zenith in the 1960s with pop art, dress, music. In architectural terms, Archigram was probably its true expression.

However, Alison and Peter Smithson were not satisfied by representations on paper. They felt that while the sculptor's maquette and the artist's sketch were satisfying as communications in their own right, drawings and models did not provide that level of satisfaction for the architect. The Smithsons' contention was that only a building can provide the expression of the architect's art, and that inventive buildings were being restricted by regulation in a way that pop art or sculpture were not (Dunster 1982). There could be an alternative interpretation. First, from the outside it may appear that the sculptor and artist are fulfilled by maquettes and sketches. The perception from the inside might be quite different. Secondly, design drawings may not take on significance unless they actually express the creativity in the thinking process. If they just appear as the skeleton of an idea, then possibly there is no chance of artistic communication. On the elevation of the Economist Building, the surroundings are shown quite carefully. Together with the respect for existing scale and the external spaces, this drawing conveys a good impression of the proposals.

The period of the Thin Straight Lines came and went. Whether or not it was an aberration is open to debate. However, before and after it, there continued a tradition that finds its origins in the 19th century *Artists' Pictures*. These representations have always impressed lay-clients and the public. Architects have generally been more diffident about them, possibly because they are often not produced by the architects but are the work of professional illustrators. There is a feeling that the Thin Straight Lines were drawn by architects for the benefit of their peers and themselves, whereas Realistic Impressions have wider appeal. They open architectural design to public discussion as the accessibility of these depictions enables everybody to have an opinion. Some architects and critics believe that opinion should be educated and that it is not appropriate for just anyone to have a view. They do not believe in citizens voting for proposed additions to their town or city. There is an alternative approach in which more enlightened architects try to involve their clients in the process. This may offer clients greater ownership of the design.

8.0   View of Fouracre, West Green, Hampshire
Ernest Newton 1902

Chapter 8 **Realistic Impressions**

8.1   Perspective of Sanderson Factory, Barley Mow Passage, Chiswick, London.
CFA Voysey 1902

In 1902, Harold Sanderson appointed **CFA Voysey** as the designer for an extension to their main factory. This building design appeared as the antithesis of the famous houses. It looked like a functional rectangular box which was emphasized by the white glazed bricks, used to reflect the light. The roof form that had been the essential expression of the house designs was hidden behind a parapet wall. An amusing feature is the railway carriage linking the two façades at third floor level. This was Voysey's only factory and the style is unlike any of his extensive portfolio of buildings. Yet it is not an aberration. There are similar features on the drawings of both the Lincoln Grammar School and the Carnegie Library at Limerick. These projects demonstrate an embryonic urban style that was sadly only fulfilled at Chiswick (Hitchmough 1995). The design was completed within Voysey's main period of exhibiting at the Royal Academy. However, the illustrated perspective is by the architect and there was no watercolour by Howard Gaye for exhibition purposes (see Fig. 4.18). Perhaps Voysey felt that a factory was not an appropriate subject or that the style would be too shocking.

Also around the turn of the century, **Charles H Reilly** was starting to become well known in the academic world. Architects such as Ernest Newton, CFA Voysey and Reilly took their lead from such as Norman Shaw and Ernest George, although the American style was imported into Liverpool through Reilly's own enthusiasm for it. The establishment of full-time courses in architecture at provincial and metropolitan institutions gathered pace in the early years of the century. Drawing was used as a design tool rather than an end in itself. In a number of Schools, such as the Architectural Association, Arts and Crafts predominated. At Liverpool, Reilly literally threw all this away and other Schools soon followed. He introduced the grand manner of the Beaux Arts, as practised by the French and Americans. The end products of much labour became beautifully rendered measured drawings of buildings or original designs. This systematic approach enhanced professionalism but lost spontaneity and the Britishness of the Arts and Crafts. In establishing his dominance at Liverpool, Reilly set a pattern that endured for half a century. He opened the way for international influences from which there was no going back.

8.2   View of the Entrance, Competition Entry for Liverpool Anglican Cathedral
CH Reilly 1903

The influence of modern America was unavoidable and to the younger generation, its architects such as Daniel H Burnham made a strong impression. Although his work in Chicago was considered vulgar by some, its principles started to appear in Britain. Promoted as Chicago comes to London, Selfridge's Department Store in Oxford Street demonstrates the grand American scale through Beaux Arts classicism (Fellows 1995). It has already been shown in Chapter 5 that Reilly considered the architect **Cyril Farey** (1888–1954) to be the best architectural draughtsman and critic in 1930s Britain. He produced wonderful drawings and he was not short of a few opinions. There is almost an echo of the debate over Christopher Wren in Farey's observation that a facility to design does not necessarily accompany a gift for draughtsmanship and vice versa. He wrote that it may generally be assumed that if a clever architect does not draw, it is not because he cannot but because he declines to do so. Yet, it is not always the case. There have always been distinguished practitioners who convey to their assistants, designs for buildings by means of sketches that seem little better than scribbles, which are put neatly

8.3   Perspective of Selfridge's Department Store, Oxford Street, London
Cyril Farey for Burnham, Swales, Atkinson, Burnet 1907

on to paper for the architects to consider the result. The argument is that such practitioners have concentrated attention on design, from which they may become distracted if having to undertake the laborious duties of drawing as well. It is interesting that Farey assumes perspective views will always be set up to visualize a proposed building and its relationship to its neighbours; and frequently interiors will also need to be illustrated by perspective as well. His assertion is that a real architect combines design and illustration for his client while the philosophical architect gets others to illustrate the design for him. Farey himself was as much an illustrator of designs by others, as he was an architect. He developed a glorious watercolour style that must have been the envy of his contemporaries, and thus was engaged by some famous architects to illustrate their equally famous work. It is fascinating to speculate whether he would regard some of them as philosophical. He actually used the same exciting watercolour style to illustrate existing architecture in a topographical sense.

At the time, it must have been clear which were design drawings and which were from life. However, in retrospect there is a certain ambiguity. For example, his impression of the Imperial Hotel in Japan looks like it could be a representation of the design. Yet, it is hard to believe that Frank Lloyd Wright would have commissioned him when he had already produced his own large and detailed aerial perspective. The date seems to confirm the British version as a topographical painting. Cyril was in no doubt that if a client is going to spend a lot of money on a building, it is legitimate to ask for a realistic impression of the intended building. He is also quite clear that failure to do so is definitely misleading. Moreover, if the failure is deliberate it may be described as fraudulent. He continues that there is no room for artistic licence and the draughtsman is not at liberty to idealize the architectural subject. Interestingly, he also notes that while an architect has a duty to make the representation of the building as realistic as he can, he would be wasting his time if he were to draw too realistic trees or people – claiming that such a duality in convention is entirely justified in logic.

8.4   View of Imperial Hotel, Tokyo
Cyril Farey 1929

8.5   View of Benson Court, Magdalene College, Cambridge.
Cyril Farey for Edwin Lutyens 1928

8.6   Watercolour of Liverpool Roman Catholic Cathedral
Cyril Farey for Edwin Lutyens 1930

According to Margaret Richardson, **Edwin Lutyens**' office did not generally do perspectives. He used William Walcot and Cyril Farey as his perspective artists. In the early days, Lutyens preferred Walcot but later came to employ Farey much more. He is reported to have said that the watercolours were so real that you could walk into a Farey building (Richardson 1994). Others have noted how in the watercolours of Liverpool Cathedral, the combination of architect and illustrator captured the grace and strength of this great design (Schaller 1997). As with the designs of Richard Meier, the unbuilt is no less real than a finished building. Farey himself felt that his representations at Liverpool were of special interest. This was not only because of the subject but also because they proved how a very precise method of draughtsmanship can demonstrate the qualities of a romantic design (Farey and Edwards 1931). The view of Benson Court has understandably received much less attention. In some ways, it is even more precise and the reflection of the buildings in the water certainly adds to the artistic effect. It generates a kind of grand formality without losing the notion that these are real buildings.

8.7   Front View, Raffles College, Singapore
Cyril Farey and Graham R Dawbarn 1917

8.8   Design for a West End Club, London
Cyril Farey c. 1918

Farey acknowledges that his attitude to architectural drawing may seem hard on the artist who rejoices in displaying his own personality but it must be remembered that the art of architecture takes precedence over that of draughtmanship. The essential interest is a prediction of the appearance of a building, not some strange version of it that may tickle the fancy of an individual artist. He suggested that a person genuinely interested in architecture would prefer to see a bad drawing of a well designed building than a superb drawing of a badly designed one (Farey and Edwards 1931). It is sad if that is the choice, and indeed quite ironic that Farey should be so supportive of the late 19th and early 20th century competitions. He referred to them as great, especially in the obligatory requirement for a perspective. One of his favourites was the representation of an unsuccessful design for the London County Hall Competition. Perhaps not even Farey could resist being seduced by a magnificent drawing. Its creator was **Edwin A Rickards** (1872–1920) who was a superb draughtsman with a natural flair for Baroque details and an intuitive approach to design.

He entered into partnership with **James Stewart** (1856–1904) and **Henry V Lanchester** (1863–1953). Lanchester, Stewart and Rickards had almost unparalleled success in competition designs for public buildings. They seemed to have their fingers on the pulse, with schemes in the grand manner on a modest scale. Rickards' realistic representations of the buildings must also have played an important role in their success. He was able to produce marvellously fluent drawings which looked like they could have been directly translated from paper into reality. Unfortunately for them, the style soon began to look old fashioned and idiosyncratic itself and by 1910, they had lost the spirit of the times. There was a suspicion that slick and mannered draughtsmanship had outgrown the architecture it was supposed to represent. The Beaux Arts and modern America hastened a radical change that began to spread through the English architectural scene. It spelled the end, at least for many decades, of the English picturesque design tradition and laid the path for eventual outbreak of continental modernism (Fellows 1995 and 1998).

8.9   Competition Entry for London County Hall, Lambeth
Edwin Rickards 1907

8.10   Competition Entry for the Board of Trade Building, Embankment Gardens, London
Edwin Rickards c. 1908

Giles Gilbert Scott (1880–1960) was well selected by Reilly for his book *Representative British Architects of Today, 1931.* Architect of Cambridge University Library, Liverpool Anglican Cathedral, Waterloo Bridge and designer of the much loved GPO telephone boxes, he was highly regarded as the link between traditionalism and modernism. Scott was one of the very few who could produce architecture that was acceptable to modernists as well as traditionalists, and could handle the design of huge new building types. Surprisingly, he had no formal education at a School of Architecture nor any technical training beyond his articled pupillage with Temple Moore, a designer of Gothic churches. Yet Scott became associated with a building so closely identified with modernism, it could have been an icon of the Italian Futurists. In 1934, Charles Reilly was one of many who called Battersea Power Station *a new cathedral* – much to the architect's annoyance. In fact Scott was not the original architect. He was engaged in 1930 to improve the bland brick elevations by J Theo Halliday of Halliday and Agate. The strength and solidity of the design are well represented by this drawing.

Battersea was the result of collaboration and compromise. After the 1930s success seemed to allude him. He continued to work but the post-war architectural world would care less for his style and sense of drama. Scott was one of the last in a generation of *art architects* (AD 10 November 1979) and post-war Britain was poorer for it. By the late 1950s, even the Royal College of Art was being described as a collection of shacks. Clearly a new building was needed and as the College had so much architectural talent, it was decided that it should be an inside job. **Hugh Casson** (1910–99) and two old friends, HT Cadbury-Brown and Robert Gooden, were chosen. Gooden seems to have taken quite a minor role and Casson was happy enough to act as overseer and lend his name. So, it was (Jim) Cadbury-Brown who took main responsibility for the workload. However, Casson was an inveterate artist and, almost in the mould of Hugh Ferris, would continually draw out the design as it was debated. He produced numerous concept sketches on a paper roll. His partner Neville Conder could never remember seeing him use a T-square or parallel rule (Manser 2000).

8.11 View of Battersea Power Station, London
AC Webb for Giles Gilbert Scott 1931

8.12 View of Extension to the Royal College of Art, South Kensington, London
Hugh Casson c. 1959

Richard (Robin) **Seifert** (b 1910) established one of the most successful architectural practices in mid 20th century Britain. The designs were startling, dynamic, spectacular and generally large. He was an opportunist who developed an expertise in concrete as a structural and expressed material at a time when brick and stone were difficult to obtain. He also pioneered the alliance between developer and architect in commercial building. During the 1960s and 1970s, it seemed that hardly a week went by without the announcement of another proposal from architects R Seifert and Partners. They produced flats, houses, hotels, conference centres, banks and above all speculative offices. There were schemes all over Britain but principally they changed the face of London. In his own estimation, Seifert was working within the genre of Walter Gropius (Morgan and Naylor 1987) as some kind of successor. To the public, he was the man who proliferated the commercial block in British cities (AJ 22 August 1973). John Betjeman was the figurehead of a growing nostalgia for an England in better days. People began to feel out of sympathy with the austere and anonymous. To Betjeman, these were symbolized by Lieutenant Colonel Seifert (Esher 1981). The dates attributed to the two drawings are done so very cautiously. Stylistically, it just seems that the first is from the 1960s, whereas the second is probably an early 1970s design. In fact, they are rather anonymous office developments but the style of the depictions by AF Gill is interesting. It comes from an era that emphasized the gloss of reflection. Often, even more could be gained from pools of water on the ground.

8.13 Perspective of Office Development, London
AF Gill for R Seifert and Partners
c. 1965

8.14 Perspective of Office Development, London
AF Gill for R Seifert and Partners
c. 1970

The reasons for the vitriolic greeting by the architectural press to the **Demetri Porphyrios** (b 1949) entry for the Inland Revenue Offices competition are not immediately clear. In a local newspaper poll, the people of Nottingham voted this scheme the winner. However, they were not the judges. There may have been a kind of snobbery associated with it – as if the notion of ordinary people judging fine architecture is ridiculous. After all, what do they know about it? There is also a condescending tone in which the metropolitan elite is grudgingly agreeing to save the provincials from themselves. The main damning criticism is that the scheme is not modern. It is certainly the only submission that felt like it belonged in the context. One interesting thought is whether the realistic impression also antagonized the critics. The comments about cheating with the scale are difficult to assess without knowing the detailed requirements more fully, but many modern buildings can provide relatively little accommodation in relation to their bulk. Moreover, as Quinlan Terry has shown at Richmond Riverside, the needs of present day offices can be met by traditional styles and extremely pleasant spaces can be achieved as well.

A sample critique of this proposal is as follows: *One project, that of Demetri Porphyrios, was clearly a rogue submission. Three of the five drawings were perspectives of what looks like a hallowed Oxbridge College which has grown since its foundation. The proposal offers a series of collegiate courts planned loosely on the site implicitly raising the status of the humble tax collector. The style of Porphyrios' scheme may have won the hearts and minds of the good people of Nottingham but, fortunately for the modernists if not the locals, the assessors are made of sterner stuff. The architect has assembled a variety of similarly scaled building blocks, detailed in brick and stone, and predictably squashed together in a tudor-bethan style that would be reassuringly familiar to the men from the suburbs who might come to work there. The sleight of hand which the perspectivists' of Porphyrios and fellow schemes demonstrated at Paternoster Square have been employed again here. The buildings which are in reality, mostly five-storey lumps of municipal accommodation are scaled down or concealed by oversized planting to demonumentalize and domesticate them. Such a presentation offers an enlightening glimpse into the psyche of the historicists. Their mission ultimately goes beyond a drive to conceal modern reality behind a stylistically friendly cloak; they would have the cloak itself reduced to a point of invisibility, 'look'– they may say, 'isn't it wonderful, you'll hardly notice it's there.' Fortunately, in this case, it isn't going to be.* (AJ 26 February 1992). One is reminded of Quinlan Terry's description of his own office. It used to be a house, then a shop and now it is an office. One of the great things about traditional architecture is its flexibility, which adds to its longevity.

8.15   View from the Castle, Inland Revenue Offices, Nottingham
Demetri Porphyrios 1992

During the 1980s, **Jeremy Dixon** (b 1939) completed three distinctive housing schemes in London. The projects at St Mark's Road, North Kensington (1975–80), Lanark Road, Maida Vale (1982) and Dudgen's Wharf, Isle of Dogs (1986–88) succeeded in pulling together the historic and modern traditions (Glancey 1989). The picture of the docklands housing conjures images of Sunday leisure – walking, fishing, relaxing, admiring the view, and there is an atmosphere of John Constable about the composition of trees, buildings and people. The feeling of tranquility is assisted by an expanse of water in the foreground, leaving no doubt as to the setting but, at the same time, providing a space that maintains distance to the observer. Meanwhile, a competition for alterations to the Royal Opera House was held in 1983. Building Design Partnership teamed-up with Dixon to realize the project, which was finally approved in 1991. The painting of the proposed Opera House is a remarkable contribution to architectural illustration. The artistic reaction to an architectural representation such as this one is that its realism could equally well be captured by a camera. The first obvious response is that it is a design drawing and therefore the scene has never actually happened. Part of the skill of this artist is that he leads viewers to believe that they are looking at a real event when of course they are not. The people are real enough, some of them are quite recognisable as individuals. The place exists, although not in this form. The wonder that is created combines the people, the place and the proposed architecture together in a seamless way. There is something slightly medieval about its character. Clowns and acrobats among the throng capture a feeling for times gone by. There is also a tension in the air. People in costume are unpredictable and slightly menacing as the

outer expression may be different from that inside. The picture becomes a contrast of playfulness and apprehension, emphasized by the voyeurs on the high balcony. This representation is much more than the illustration of an intended building. It is a modern-day scene in the style of Gandy or Canaletto. Both of these paintings show the buildings in realistic settings with people using the spaces in a natural way. Not only are these the kind of impressions that clients and the public can understand but also they engender a wish to see them realized with the least possible delay.

8.16   River View of Dudgen's Wharf, Isle of Dogs, London
Carl Laubin for Jeremy Dixon and Edward Jones 1986

8.17 *(overleaf)* **Alterations to the Royal Opera House, Covent Garden, London**
Carl Laubin for Jeremy Dixon with BDP and Edward Jones 1983

Sometimes it feels that controversial competitions were as prevalent at the end of the 20th century as they were at the end of the 19th. A notorious one in recent times was the Extension to the National Gallery. By September 1992, seven schemes had been shortlisted from the original seventy entries (AJ 15 September 1982). In January, editorials were starting to appear, making reference to this *ailing architectural competition* (AJ 5 January 1983). In a show of solidarity, the RIBA exhibited nearly all the schemes in an attempt to confirm that the winners had been correctly judged (AJ 2 February 1983). By May 1984, it was finally decided that a conclusion must be brought to the whole affair by the end of the month. Peter Ahrends was starting to reveal in interviews that the competition and public inquiry had become a significant ordeal (AJ 2 May 1984). In April 1985, it was proclaimed that the competition saga had ended when Lord Annan, chairman of the trustees and instigator of the competition, announced that a new development was to be funded by the Sainsbury family and the winning scheme by ABK had been scrapped (AJ 10 April 1985).

Trying to side step all the claims and counter-claims, the illustrated entry by Richard Seifert and Partners did not get past the first stage. However, it is compelling as a beautifully drawn sequence moving along Trafalgar Square. Also shown is the last in the series of Alban Gate drawings, which is a realistic ground level view. There is a clear aim to demonstrate the human scale of what otherwise is quite a monumental project. This low level perspective is precisely drawn in ink and coloured pencil and perhaps surprisingly without shadow.

8.18   Competition Entry for Extension to the National Gallery, Trafalgar Square, London
R Seifert and Partners 1982

8.19   View of Lee House, Alban Gate, London
Terry Farrell and Partners 1987
(see Figs 5.17, 6.13)

**8.20   Watercolour of a Private
Residence, Naples, Florida**
TW Schaller for Richard Meier 1995

Tom Schaller's objective in architectural drawing is to provide a synthesis between the objective and subjective. As an architect, he understands the properties of a proposed design, and as an artist, he can bring out the more emotive qualities. In the description of this watercolour of a design by **Richard Meier**, the point is well made about understanding the essential idea and using it in the representation. In this case it is the contrast between the lush natural greenery, and the technical precision and formality, in the elements of the building. Schaller implores would-be designers to think with a pencil, although he admits that in fact the pencil could be a pen, a brush or even a computer screen. He highlights the larger process of creative thinking as more significant than any one drawing, painting or finished building (Schaller 1997). Rob Becker's philosophy is the use of images to tell a story through atmosphere. Interestingly, he often involves the client in a kind of conversation which permits the client to become part of the process that brings the images to life. Once again, the main medium is watercolour.

Rob relates that especially in competition work, impressions are often needed very quickly, and based on scant design information. In the Four Seasons Hotel competition, apart from fax and email, there was no communication except a total of ten minutes in telephone conversations. These focused entirely on the atmosphere which was summarized as very serene with absolutely no red. The second round required three images in four days, based on a design that had barely developed. Nevertheless, it proved to be a successful formula.

**8.21   View of the Lobby – Winning Entry,
International Competition, Four
Seasons Hotel and Luxury
Apartments, Beirut, Lebanon**
Robert Becker for Kohn Pederson Fox
1998

Realistic impressions and models are equally fascinating for clients and the public. Nevertheless, the use of models has seemingly been played down in the analysis of architectural representation. From the Renaissance, through Modernism to the present day, it is clear that a multitude of architects have used them as design tools. There is a constant image of the Greats from any era, moulding pieces of wood, card or plastic as they tested the latest idea for a design. Models have also won both commissions and competitions for their designers. Aspects from the three dimensional distribution of spaces to the transparency of the envelope have often been shown to their best advantage in a model. The debate centres on the appearance. While some are stripped down to show a typical bay, structural form or spatial relationship, others try to achieve scaled-down reality. It is perhaps this last group that creates the unease. The model has moved from an analytical tool or explanatory device, to a kind of parody of the intended building and its design. It is almost the equivalent of the relationship between chocolate box painting and art.

9.0   St Paul's Wesleyan Church, Bowden, Manchester
William Brakspear c. 1850

Models have a surprisingly long history but from the mid 20th century they became even more representative of real buildings – with trees, cars and people around them. Models are often admired as they enable everybody to visualize the proposals from all directions. Yet, they have also been criticized in at least two respects. One aspect is that it is claimed they disguise the large scale of some modern buildings. Generally models are viewed from above which produces less impact than from the human viewpoint. Another factor is that they imply a neatness in the environment that can never be replicated in practice. According to Cyril Farey, the principal function of the architectural model is to supplement the perspective sketch and represent the perspective view of a building or group of buildings in a more obvious and spectacular form than is possible with a drawing. Also, the model has the advantage that it is the pictorial equivalent of not only one sketch but very many. By walking around the model one may obtain innumerable views of the building that it represents. He felt that clients greatly appreciate the consideration shown to them when a model of the proposed building is prepared for their inspection, and in the case of significant projects, a large model is undoubtedly the best method of representing the design (Farey and Edwards 1931). Many three dimensional forms are difficult to depict in drawings and are too elaborate to be accurately shown in a few renderings. There is ample evidence that important commissions using these forms sometimes require hundreds of design models. It is estimated that the number of sketches needed to achieve the same results would be in the thousands (Hohauser 1970). In addition, different options can be slotted into a model of the context for comparison.

During the Gothic period, architects in most of Europe were developing drawings as the principal means of communication. At the same time in Italy, models were becoming more prevalent. While the simpler churches and palaces could be illustrated by drawings, models were used to stimulate clients' imaginations at a time when every major building design was striving to be original, exceptional and colossal. Some of the models were quite big too. For S Petronio in Bologna (c. 1390), a twelfth scale example was constructed in stone and plaster. It measured fifty-three feet in length and not surprisingly was broken up in 1406. During the 15th century, models became more familiar as the new style of the Early Renaissance had to justify its appearance. Due to its intrinsic laws, the style was especially suitable for representation in this way. Moreover, many of the architects had begun as wood workers and could therefore make models easily. Brunelleschi constantly used models. For the dome of Florence Cathedral, he made several – from a small one that he could carry under his cloak to the largest, in brick. It was only with these models that the necessary conviction and enthusiasm could be generated. The remains of several of them are still preserved today. As with everything else, Alberti had very distinct views on this subject. He cautioned everyone against models that are adorned with decoration, adding that they are only fit for vain and ambitious people to impose upon the ignorant. His strongly held view was that only *modelli nudi e semplici* offer proof of the genius of the designer (Burckhardt 1987). It is a recurring theme that models which try to mimic reality are less successful than those that do not. Alberti wrote: *I therefore always highly commend the ancient custom of builders, who . . . in real models of wood and other substances, examined*

the whole work . . . I must not omit to observe that the making of curious polished models, with the delicacy of painting, is not required . . . but is rather the part of the vain architect that makes it his business . . . to divert him from a rigorous examination . . . For this reason I would not have models too exactly finished nor too delicate and neat but plain and simple, more to be admired for the contrivance of the inventor than the hand of the workman. Between the design of the painter and that of the architect, there lies this difference that the painter by the exactness of his shades, lines and angles, endeavours to make the parts seem to rise from the canvas. Whereas the architect . . . makes his relieves from the design . . . not by the apparent perspective but by the real compartments founded upon reason (Alberti 1485). Historically, models were carried from patron to patron and town to town. Due to the crudity of drafting, difficulties in fast reproduction of drawings and widespread illiteracy, many buildings were constructed by taking measurements directly from these detailed design models (Hohauser 1970). Michelangelo continually instructed models to be made and they almost took on a life of their own. His model for the stairs of the Laurenziana (1539) travelled in *a little box* to Florence from Rome. Voyaging in the opposite direction was Vasari with his wooden model of the alterations to the Palazzo della Signoria. The exacting Cosimo I had commanded him to take the model to Michelangelo, so that the latter might be able to judge the proposals (Burckhardt 1987). As a technique, modelling is infinitely flexible. Amongst other uses, it can be employed by architects to test their ideas during the design process, it can be an invaluable aid to three dimensional thinking and it can be a record of the agreed building design.

9.1   Exterior of the Great Model, St Paul's Cathedral, London
Christopher Wren 1673
(see Figs 3.10, 3.11, 3.12)

On 12 November 1673, Charles II issued a detailed commission for the rebuilding of the Cathedral Church of St Paul, London. The commission confirmed that the objective was to produce a cathedral that would become a principal ornament of the City and the King's realm. From designs that **Christopher Wren** had presented to the King, one was selected. A significant point in the commission is that the King commanded a model to be made of this design. It was to be so large and exact that it might remain as a perpetual and unchangeable rule for the direction and conduct of the whole work (Wren Society 1936). The Great Model, as it became known, was made by William Cleere over the winter of 1673–4 (Summerson 1953). The design took place over the previous spring and summer as a thorough reworking of the Greek Cross Plan, with the addition of a portico and assembly vestibule. The cost of the model was over £500 and it represents a design said by Wren's son in *Parentalia* to be the Surveyor's favourite (Hart 1995). In 1673, Wren must have felt that he had reached an unassailable position. He had been commissioned by the King to rebuild St Paul's with his favourite Greek Cross design, he was knighted and made the most public declaration of his intentions for the Cathedral with the Great Model – just as the King had commanded. However, perhaps he underestimated the influence of the clergy. The objections were that it was not only too European but too Popish, and specifically too much like St Peter's in Rome. Moreover, it was insufficiently cathedral-like. There was an overwhelming desire to emphasize the Church of England and differentiate it from the Church of Rome by adopting a Latin Cross Plan. Wren was forced to abandon the design. The Great Model remains as a *perpetual and unchangeable* reproach for what might have been (Downes 1988). The combination of Charles II's intention for instructing the model to be made, the fact that the design at that stage is referred to as the Great Model and that it still exists – are all testaments to the power of modelling as a representation of architectural design. There is also a downside. The rejection of the Great Model by the clergy was very public as well. Wren entered a period of despair and cynicism. Never again did he make such an open declaration of his proposals, leaving people generally unaware of a design until the building was constructed.

9.2   Interior of the Great Model, St Paul's Cathedral, London
Christopher Wren 1673
(see Figs 3.10, 3.11, 3.12)

The model of St Martin's, designed by **James Gibbs**, is stunning in its polished hardwood. The detail is phenomenal and it looks as fresh and crisp at the beginning of the 21st century as it must have done when new. Tyringham (1792–1800) for William Praed is the largest of eighteen completely new houses designed by **John Soane** during his career. This is a fine example of a client model made in mahogany by Joseph Parkins from design drawings supplied by Soane. It was put together at quite an early stage of the process, as the tribune or inner hall was not yet finalized. It is a sophisticated piece of work divided horizontally into three layers, to show the interiors. The model is part of a comprehensive presentation of the house that includes perspectives of the entrance façade from the garden as well as the interior of the hall. All are watercolours painted by Joseph Michael Gandy (Richardson and Stevens 1999). The ingenuity of this model enables both the exterior and interior of the design proposals to be displayed in terms of form and distribution of spaces. The paintings complete the impression by offering context and decoration.

9.3   St Martin's in the Fields, London
St James Gibbs c. 1720
(see Fig. 3.14)

9.4   Tyringham, Buckinghamshire
John Soane 1793–4

9.5   Bank Stock Office, Bank of England, London

John Soane 1793

(see Figs 4.1, 4.3)

9.6   Tivoli Corner, Bank of England, London

John Soane 1805

(see Figs 4.1, 4.3)

An impressive number of design models were produced for various parts of the Bank of England. Joseph Parkins was again the maker of the design model for the Bank Stock Office. This time, it is in painted wood, copper and yellow glass. In order to lighten the innovative non-combustible superstructure and to maximize illumination, Soane and his mentor **George Dance The Younger** (1741–1825) designed a pyramidal composition of attenuated arches, vaults, clerestories, a pendentive dome and a circular iron lantern. The objective of the model was to assess the office's proportions, stability and lighting effects (Richardson and Stevens 1999). In many respects, it looks like a more modern structural model. It would not be too far fetched to see these forms as a house design in concrete by Le Corbusier. The Tivoli Corner was designed several times and was modelled at least twice. The *circular* design model in painted wood represents the final version. It combines Grecian simplicity, Roman monumentality and Baroque massing in a way that it is considered by some to be Soane's greatest masterpiece (Richardson and Stevens 1999).

9.7   Viceroy's Palace, New Delhi. 1920
Remade into the Architect's Face.
1931
Edwin Lutyens and Office

9.8   Bank of England, London
Herbert Baker 1930

In 1911–12, two capital cities of the Empire were proposed. The Canberra competition was won by an architect from Chicago but New Delhi became the responsibility of **Edwin Lutyens**. Both were built on Beaux Arts principles. As president of the RIBA, Reginald Blomfield had proposed Lutyens, hoping that Lutyens would return the favour and appoint him as an associate. He actually chose **Herbert Baker** (1862–1946), a fellow pupil from Ernest George's office (Fellows 1995). However, the infamous row with Lutyens, and the *bumptious* rebuilding of Soane's Bank of England contributed to a perception of Baker as a villain in Reilly's book *Representative British Architects of Today, 1931*. In the early attempts at a Brave New World, Lutyens became like a much loved whimsical old uncle whereas Baker just seemed like someone from the past, best forgotten (AD 10 November 1979). Baker seems to be especially outdated when the buildings of **Frank Lloyd Wright** are recalled. Even the Robie House from 1907 appears modern. He may have been the master of space (Blake 1963) but some of his built forms are rather special too. Drexler (1962) concentrates on Wright's drawings. This is understandable with such quantity as well as quality. In all the innumerable books about Wright, it is actually quite difficult to find illustrations of any models. It is clear that Wright preferred drawings as a design and presentation tool and there is a suspicion that he had a favoured viewpoint for each of his buildings. He could also provide an atmosphere to a composition with his drawing technique. Nevertheless, the more objective representation of modelling celebrates the breathtaking forms of these designs, and should also be embraced. There is even a photograph of the Guggenheim model on which Wright has sketched some amendments to the design,

9.9   Robie House, Chicago, Illinois
Frank Lloyd Wright 1907

(see Fig. 6.2)

[reproductions included where originals lost]

9.11   Guggenheim Museum, New York
Frank Lloyd Wright c. 1951

(see Figs 5.3, 6.4)

9.10   Falling Water, Bear Run, Pennsylvania
Frank Lloyd Wright 1935

(see Fig. 6.3)

[reproductions included where originals lost]

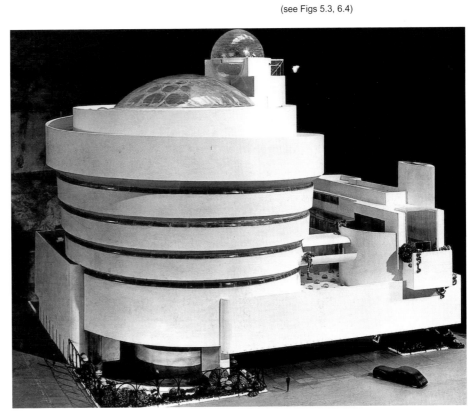

9.12   Villa Savoye, Poissy
Le Corbusier 1929
(see Fig. 7.15)
[reproductions included where originals lost]

9.13   Unité d'Habitation, Marseilles
Le Corbusier 1945

In a similar manner to Frank Lloyd Wright, there are numerous publications about **Le Corbusier** – his sketches, drawings, paintings, sculptures, and even his writings. Yet, it seems that little attention has been paid to the models of his designs. The model of the Villa Savoye perfectly captures the atmosphere of a building design that has always been considered as the apex of the *white house designs* (Ruegg 1999). It is smooth, white, planar, precise, sculptural, independent of context – and so is the building. Nevertheless, there is a strange feeling of ambiguity. It can be readily accepted that a model should be a three dimensional expression of form without hint of materials, finishes, decoration or colour. However, when the architecture expresses exactly that quality, is the model presenting an image or is it intended to be a faithful likeness? Whether or not intended, the coincidence of style between model and architecture creates a realistic impression in a way that the drawings do not. They appear as abstractions, as if trying to convey some kind of philosophical point rather than giving the clients an indication of the appearance of their planned home.

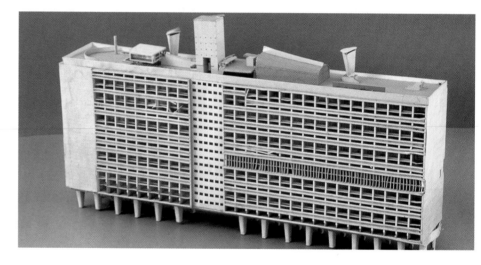

With the model of the Unité d'Habitation, there is no ambiguity. It is obviously a representation of the external appearance of the intended building. The box form ran rampant in residential construction during the second part of the 20th century. Nevertheless, this representation shows the classic features that have turned this building into a design icon. The piloti and features on the roof deck are relatively familiar. It is the depth and patterning generated by the balconies to each flat that are the essence of this design. It is well known that Le Corbusier enjoyed drawing in front of people, as a means of explaining how a particular design would work. There is also the famous photograph of him with this model of the Unité. He is clearly explaining some aspect of it. In sifting through the large volume of the photographs *Le Corbusier at work*, there are a number of him with pen in hand. For somebody who believed in people living ordered lives, there is an astonishing amount of clutter lying around the office. At first, it seems that it comprises mostly rolled-up drawings. Closer inspection reveals that in fact, there are a considerable number of models in various states of assembly and disrepair (Burri 1999).

In November 1950, Archbishop Dubourg visited Le Corbusier's atelier. He would have found a passageway on the first floor, built onto a church overlooking a courtyard. About two thirds of this corridor was occupied by main workspace, where according to Burri (1999), every surface was covered with photos, plans and models in no apparent order. The Archbishop inspected a plaster model and drawings of a design that was to become the legendary chapel at Ronchamp, but it still lacked the drama of the famous design. The circumstances surrounding the destruction of the model are not known but Le Corbusier and his assistant André Maisonnier diligently expanded the ideas until it was ready for approval in 1951. The second model was by Maisonnier himself. For the ultimate expression of sculptural concrete, modelling in hardwood might seem a peculiar choice. Le Corbusier had suggested that the towers should be made like periscopes in papier mâché (Raeburn and Wilson 1987). Yet, the warmth and charm of this depiction of the fascinating forms and pierced openings must have captivated all who were presented with it.

One of the most striking features of Maisons Jaoul is the roughness of brick and concrete. Yet, the precise, smooth whiteness of the model is almost reminiscent of the Villa Savoye. In principle, the forms at Neuilly are quite simple and should be reinforced by the repetition. In fact, they appear rather complicated and this is emphasized by the model. The symbolism of the family replicated by a family of forms is an admired technique. In this case, two members do not constitute a sufficient grouping and the design is prone to duality. A more positive interpretation is that an interesting tension is generated by two similar forms positioned at right angles to one another. Unfortunately, they are diluted by random and functional projections. The openings also appear to be random but as in most of Le Corbusier's designs, this is where his art and architecture find synthesis. Although completely white, the model seems to show the framing to the openings, even more strongly than the finished building itself. The patterning of punched holes to the side elevations and the screens at the ends exude a similarly satisfying composition to that developed by Piet Mondrian.

9.14 Maisons Jaoul, Neuilly sur Seine
Le Corbusier 1952
(see Fig. 7.16)
[reproductions included where originals lost]

9.15 Chapelle Notre Dame du Haut, Ronchamp
Le Corbusier 1951
(see Fig. 7.17)

The Festival of Britain in 1951 was advertised not only as an exhibition of modern design or indeed faith in the future, but as the autobiography of a nation. The story was told through a series of pavilions on the South Bank in London, although there were events all over the country. The Festival belonged to an era that was dominated by planning and this ethos was evident in its analysis. The exhibition pavilions were placed in a certain deliberate sequence. Within each, the displays were arranged in a certain order. There was no compulsion to view the exhibition in this sequence but there was a kind of irritation that visitors might find some of the exhibits mystifying and inconsequential if they chose their own route (Cox 1951). The Seas and Ships Pavilion was designed by **Basil Spence** (1907–1976) as a shipyard gantry with outdoor displays. The official handbook pointed out that Britain builds more ships and a greater variety of them than any other nation, and that the contemporary expression of this great tradition is on display (Banham and Hillier 1976). This pavilion stood on the very central part of the site, adjacent to the Dome of Discovery and next to the Skylon. Pavilion buildings are very significant in the development of architecture, and models could be considered as the ideal medium for their explanation. They have invariably been the expression of the latest style or technology. Most often, they were intended to be temporary and therefore permitted greater experimentation than permanent buildings. Moreover, they have not needed to respond to the realism of everyday life nor to a particular context. The assembly and disassembly have not only been important to the designs but sometimes the guiding principle. Thus the genre of exhibition buildings and its design models have a close relationship that was particularly expressed throughout the 20th century.

9.16   Summer Pavilion, Seas and Ships, Festival of Britain, London
Basil Spence 1950

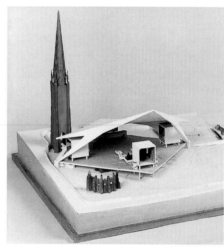

9.17   Competition Entry for Coventry Cathedral
Alison and Peter Smithson 1951

It has been suggested that for the next generation of architects, the Festival style was an anathema. A number looked for leadership to Le Corbusier or to Mies van der Rohe, with his expressed structural grid. By the time that the Festival ended, **Alison and Peter Smithson** for example, had already designed the miesian school at Hunstanton (see Fig. 7.21) and their Coventry Cathedral project. The latter was compared by David Sylvester to the Dome of Discovery, but it was never a *Festival* design like the scheme that actually took first prize in the Coventry Cathedral competition, by Basil Spence. Planned in a remarkably similar way to his

Seas and Ships Pavilion, it carried the style deep into the surprised sixties (Banham and Hillier 1976). By contrast, the Smithson's scheme was a radical departure. The form is simple, although the geometry may appear complex. It was intended to be a hyperbolic paraboloid, constructed as a concrete shell. The appearance suggests that it could be a bird about to take flight and there were allusions to the phoenix with all the symbolism that follows from it. The graceful simplicity of this form could only be clearly shown in a model. It is also the kind of model that would have pleased Alberti – *modelli nudi e semplici*.

In 1959, Harold Macmillan won the *never had it so good* election and the people of Britain realized that they were living in an affluent society. They also realized that they were on the verge of the greatest property boom in British history. Over the skyline of the West End rose the Thorn Building by Basil Spence, who was still regarded as one of the heroes of the Festival of Britain. From a viewpoint in the 21st century, one of the main reasons for constructing a design model is to show how the proposed building fits in with the existing context. As architects looked ahead to the 1960s, there were other objectives. Modernism, at that time, was an evangelical movement. The proposed development in this model is purposefully trying to startle the smaller buildings from previous times. It could even be that it is attempting to bully them, to knock them out of the way. The existing buildings easily become blighted and less valuable as they stand in the shadow of a symbol of Modernism. Before long, their maintenance becomes uneconomic and the next step is demolition, which leaves more space for the march of progress.

9.18 Thorn EMI Building, London
Basil Spence 1959

9.19 The Architect's House, Blackheath, London
Peter Moro 1957

The house that **Peter Moro** (1911–1998) designed for himself is a cool white box floating over the greenery of Blackheath. Nevertheless, it is undogmatic and friendly. He felt that design should not come from abstract ideas but an artistic effect should result from existing conditions (Emanuel 1994). The model reinforces the image of a pavilion in the park. Unlike many modern buildings, the context is important here. Moro deliberately shows that it is a corner site. He includes the streets, pavements and boundary wall, as well as the garden and house itself.

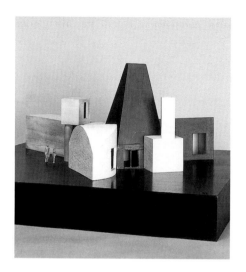

The association of **Frank Gehry** (b 1929) with artists and their thinking is consistent from his early work through to the well-known recent projects. It inspires a considered collage of unlike part with unlike part. His usual method is to make many models, to hack away at them and to glue or pin bits onto them. At a certain point, there is a sufficiently satisfactory composition to justify the production of drawings (Cook and Llewellyn-Jones 1991). The Winton Guest House is an addition to a large refined property designed by Phillip Johnson in the early 1950s. By contrast, the clients were seeking relaxation and fantasy for the visits of their children and grandchildren. The intention was that the guest house should be a collection of small differentiated building forms – a rooftop log cabin, a central hall, and so on (Arnell and Bickford 1985). This model is probably not the finished product, as there are others in existence that show the parts in greater relationship to one another. Nevertheless, it does demonstrate the variety in the composition of the design. The materials are wood, plastic and plaster. This is a deliberate choice to ensure from the onset that the parts display overtly different characters.

9.20   Winton Guest House, Wayeta, Minnesota
Frank O Gehry & Associates 1983

9.21   Federal Building and US Courthouse, Islip, New York
Richard Meier 1993

9.22   Burrell Collection, Glasgow
Barry Gasson 1971
(see Fig. 5.9)

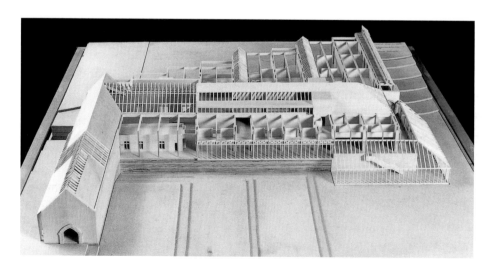

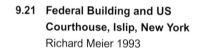

The model of the Federal Building and US Courthouse is almost as beautifully detailed as the building itself. While the design has the familiar trademarks of **Richard Meier**, for some it opens a new period of his work. This is a large building but one aspect in this phase of his career results from his increasing interest in natural climate control. One of the responses is to create a brise-soleil that reduces the scale of the main façade (Green 1999). The model of the Burrell Collection by **Barry Gasson** shows the clarity of forms and movement within the design, which were difficult to read from the drawings.

The competition model for the Centre Beaubourg (later Pompidou) by **Piano and Rogers** aptly expresses the concept. In many ways, this is not a building but more in the genre of festival pavilions. The aim was to create a public forum for interaction between people and the arts. It involves the modernist ideals of machine aesthetic, kit of parts and the feeling that it is never quite in its final form (Buchanan 1993). The model shows the external skin within which there is a second façade and hung floors. These were initially envisaged as moveable to allow the building to reform itself (Powell 1999). The model for Lloyds of London, by **Richard Rogers and Partners**, is incredibly detailed. It even displays the style of cars and people. The style of the building is probably the ultimate expression of the machine aesthetic. It is also the nearest that architectural models come to engineering prototypes. When Renzo Piano reflected on the Centre Pompidou, he concluded that it was right for the time but now looks a little like *an act of loutish bravado* (Buchanan 1993). Perhaps this partly explains why some architects started to reassert more traditional values.

9.23   Centre Culturel d'Art Georges Pompidou, Paris
Piano and Rogers 1971
(see Fig. 5.14)

9.24   Corner of Leadenhall and Lime Street: Main Entrance, Lloyds of London
Richard Rogers and Partners c. 1980
(see Figs 5.15, 6.12)

The winning competition entry by **MacCormac and Jamieson** for Worcester College, Oxford, was a scheme on three floors comprising a group of study bedrooms laid out on staggered terraces stepping back from the lake. The terraces enable the fine views to the west and south to be maximized (AJ 23 April 1980). The building is therefore low at the natural edge and rising towards the urban boundary. The rectangular grid generates a diagonal circulation route through the building (AJ 28 May 1980). The model of the levels and terraces is a three dimensional representation of the main circulation routes. The rear corner touches on the corner of Worcester Place and the front corner juts out into the lake. Thus the terraces appear as a hollow pyramid of space. The overall composition can be viewed as two wings growing out of a hub and gradually stepping back in a series of layers (AR September 1983). The plans show regular and ordered layouts, sections and elevations reveal the massing of the forms, but it is only when the model is added that the real quality of the design becomes apparent as the three dimensional experience starts to be revealed.

9.25 Worcester College, Oxford
MacCormac Jamieson Pritchard 1980
(see Figs 5.6, 5.7, 5.8)

9.26 Richmond Riverside, Surrey
Erith and Terry 1983
(see Figs 5.5, 6.0)

Despite its obvious value and strategic location, the Richmond Riverside site had become snagged in the machinery of planning for many years. The planners had insisted on some effort at diversity, appropriate to the slope of the site and the character of the area. Developers and their architects were barely emerging from the modern commercial developments epitomized by the Thorn Building. **Quinlan Terry** had always been alienated by that approach and could therefore offer a completely different philosophy, in which each building appears as a separate architectural entity within a framework.

In December 1983, the Council mounted an exhibition to consult the public about the merits of this scheme and the only other serious contender. The public voted 900 to 150 in favour of Terry's proposals, and for once a local authority responded to the public preference (Aslet 1986). Central to the exhibition, and one suspects also the decision, was the model. It has been called seductive, as if it were a word that should be used in the same context as criminal deceit. In this case, seductive means that the model expresses a design that has become an extremely attractive and worthwhile contribution to the townscape

of Richmond. As the buildings were to be occupied by different owners, it was totally reasonable to treat them in different styles. The planning constraints required a small number of buildings on the site to be conserved. The developers also wished to retain the 19th century Town Hall. This conservation work militated against a comprehensive redevelopment scheme and added more meaning to the notion of providing a variety of smaller masses. The model is very detailed and enabled all these carefully made decisions about buildings and spaces to be clearly demonstrated.

In their description of the design methodology in **Terry Farrell and Partners** office, Latham, Swenarton and Sampson (1998) explain that every significant development on a project is modelled in the workshop, sometimes time and time again. Underpinning this time-consuming process is a recognition of the limitations of the brain in dealing with complex three dimensional issues. Many architects will not admit to such a human limitation but for this practice it is not an issue, just part the process: *sketch>model>refine>define*. The presentation model for Charing Cross Station is definitely in the realistic impressions category. Indeed it is interesting to compare the photographs of the model with those of the finished building. Certainly in this case, nobody could claim that they did not know what they were getting. The low angle from which the model has been photographed is also appropriate as it is similar to the view of the building from across the river. Whether it is the feeling of looking up at the building or whether it is the night scene with light flooding out of the pierced walls as well as the giant screen, this building earns its nickname of *Palace on the River* (Binney 1991).

9.27   Charing Cross Station, Embankment Place, London
Terry Farrell and Partners 1987
(see Figs 5.19, 6.14)

9.28   International Terminal, Waterloo Station, London
Nicholas Grimshaw & Partners
c. 1988
(see Figs 5.20, 5.21)

The model of Waterloo Station by **Nicholas Grimshaw & Partners** illustrates much more of the analytical approach. There is no context or attempt to show how the building might be seen. It takes what appears to be a typical bay, once again emphasizing the explanation of this design through its cross-section. The asymmetric roof is shown as a light framework, contrasting with the main structure of the building. The imagery of the natural world has no place in this part of the presentation. This model is about structure and vertical spatial relationships.

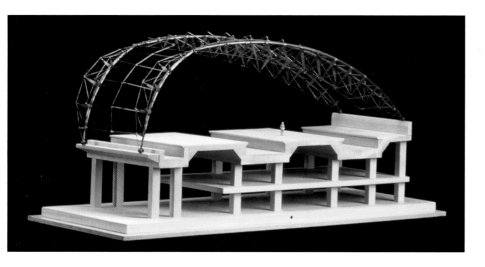

At a conference on *The Architect and the Church* held in 1960, a paper by George Pace revealed his technique for putting his ideas across to clients. He would sketch out the preliminary ideas in the clients' presence and persuade them to make their own model – thus encouraging them to identify themselves more closely with the development of the project; and not as one cynical critic put it – *help distract the clients' attention from anything they might not like in the design of the building being proposed* (Pace 1990). With the advent of Computer-Aided Design, not only would the methods and representation dramatically change but so would the language. Models became images on computer screens, dependent on rendering and software for their effect. Offices required architects to be proficient in AutoCAD Release 14 rather than pencil and watercolours. Whereas artists worked closely with architects to illustrate their schemes, new creative agencies were now offering *3D and digital media to create spatial communication*. It was right that a computer literate age should exploit new technologies to assist the design and representation of buildings.

10.0 Design for the Paternoster Square Redevelopment Scheme, London
Stephen Miller, Jeanelle Plummer, John Hare for Arup Associates 1988

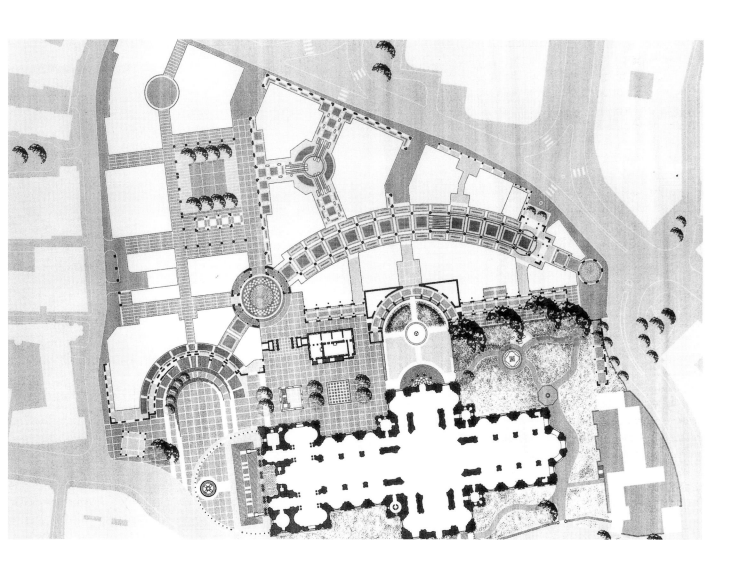

Computer-Aided Design is an application of the rapidly growing field of computer graphics. The starting point of modern interactive graphics can be traced back to 1963, to Ivan Sutherland's work on the Sketchpad drawing system (Sutherland 1963). CAD is defined as being that application of computer graphics which is used to design components and systems of mechanical, electrical, electro mechanical, and electronic devices, including structures such as buildings, automobile bodies, aeroplane and ship hulls, very large-scale-integrated (VLSI) chips, optical systems, and telephone and computer networks (Foley 1993).

Prior to the 1980s computer-aided design was run on mainframe or minicomputers mainly in large offices. Only a few people would be using CAD with most staff using drawing boards and traditional methods of design. However, the development of the graphical user interface in the late 1970s and subsequent introduction of personal computers in the early 1980s opened up the world of computer graphics to non-computer professionals. The usability of Apple Macintosh computers and the development of commercially available software accelerated the use of computers in architectural offices during the 1980s. Small and medium sized practices found it easier to invest in PC-based CAD than larger organizations, which had to decide to abandon mainframe or minicomputer systems. During the 1980s an increasing number of applications were developed and made available to architects. Although some software was developed specifically for architects, the high costs of software development and upgrade resulted in the development of *multi-purpose* software that could meet the needs of several professions.

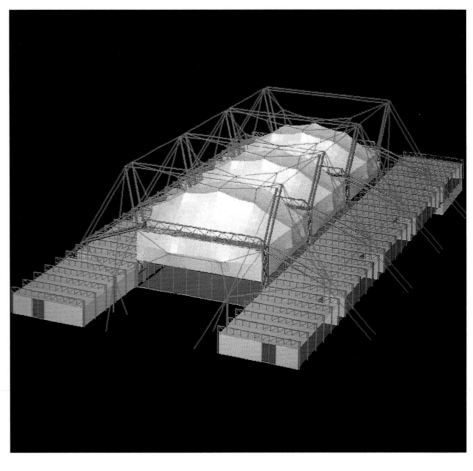

10.1   Axonometric View of Schlumberger Centre, Cambridge
Michael Hopkins and Partners 1981

Michael Hopkins and Partners used computer-aided design for the Schlumberger Centre (1979–81). The use of axonometry for 3D modelling, combined with 3D shading, detailed the relationship between the fabric roof, steel masts and other elements of this commercial research laboratory.

The RIBA Drawing Collection has an interesting archive of CAD drawings from 1989. The drawings and renderings in this collection had been submitted as competition entries in the Construction Industry Computing Association (CICA) Computer Drawing Awards. An early exhibit in the collection is a plan by **Arup Associates** who used computer-aided design in 1988 to create plans and perspectives for the Paternoster Square redevelopment scheme in London. At that time the practice used a McDonnell Douglas GDS system. Proposals for this scheme were displayed in an exhibition staged in the crypt of St Paul's Cathedral in an attempt to involve the public in this major building project (Swenarton 1988). The Association for Computer-Aided Design in Architecture (ACADIA) was formed in the early 1980s to facilitate communication and critical thinking regarding computing in architecture.

Three leading Modernist architects, Yorke, Rosenberg and Mardall, founded their partnership in 1944. Later known as **YRM**, the practice used computer-aided design extensively in the early 1980s and has kept an impressive archive of their earlier work. The Snow Hill project was the design for an office building in Birmingham. YRM's scheme maximized the office space on an awkward, sloping 1.2-hectare site just east of Snowhill Station. The design arranged 134,000 square metres of offices and related accommodation, comprising a variety of business units as well as conference facilities, along a new public space leading off the square. The 3D model for this scheme was done in Microstation and visualized in Intergraph ModelView using a network of Intergraph Interpro 340. Perspectives from this project won the Merit Award, 3D modelling category in the CICA CAD Drawing Award 1992. Views of the 3D model were generated from different viewpoints, facilitating discussion between architects and clients on the various design options. The editing facilities available in software at that time could be effectively used in the representation of multi-storey buildings with many repetitive details.

YRM also produced a 3D computer model of Whitefriars, a project to redevelop the News International printing works site in Fleet Street. The project involved the construction of new offices and retail space behind grade 2 buildings. The project lay within the Fleet Street Conservation Area and comprised 26,250 square metres of office accommodation clad externally in granite and metal skin looking inwards into a glazed atrium. The 3D computer model of the building and its neighbourhood was also done in Microstation and visualized in Intergraph ModelView using a network of Intergraph Interpro 340 workstations. To study shadows cast by neighbouring buildings, yet to avoid excessive rendering times, neighbouring buildings were represented very simply. The extrusion of 2D polygons from Ordnance Survey data, hand digitized from maps at that time, provided 3D wireframe models for subsequent rendering.

Although computer-aided design was being adopted by larger architectural practices in the early 1990s, it was primarily used for 2D drafting by a minority of staff. The Construction Industry Computer Exhibition and Conference provided insights into new developments of the time (Ray-Jones 1990) but working practices had yet to be changed for computer-aided design to be used throughout an organization. The 2D draughting entries in the CICA CAD competition did not appear to use the additional features offered by software, but only to reproduce manual draughting techniques (CICA 1991).

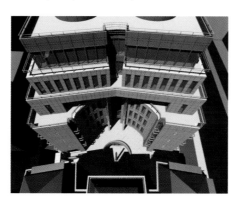

10.2   Rendered Views of Snowhill, Birmingham
Hugh Whitehead, Linda Scott for YRM 1990

10.3   Aerial Views of Whitefriars, London
Hugh Whitehead for YRM 1990

The practice of **Skidmore** (1897–1962) **Owings** (1903–84) **and Merrill** (1896–1975) submitted several drawings for the CICA/CAD drawing awards in the early 1990s. One entry simulated the effect of sunlight and shadow on Dockland Square Garden, Canary Wharf Phase II, Tower Hamlets, London. The software used was AES, a modelling system from IBM. Simulation of sunlight and shadows became an integrated feature of CAD systems in future years, using latitude of building and position of sun as input. Ability to simulate light and shade became an increasingly used facility.

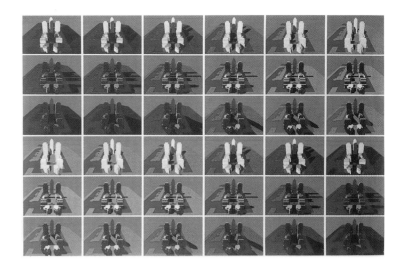

Daylighting simulation software called Radiance was developed to aid architects in environmental analysis (Ward 1994) but towards the end of the 1990s daylighting simulation tools were mainly used by a few specialists and a large proportion of practising architects continued to use hand calculations (Aizlewood and Littlefair 1996). The early 1990s confirmed the popularity of AutoCAD software in architectural practice. Released initially in 1982, subsequent versions had incorporated numerous facilities to improve speed of operation and functionality. Several major software companies had focused on the development of one core product, resulting in many third-party developers writing extensions to basic products to meet the needs of different industries. AutoCAD AEC was one such product for architects, released initially in 1988, but consistently updated to maintain compatibility with each new release of AutoCAD. Graphisoft's ArchiCAD, introduced in the mid-1980s, always had a specific focus on architecture, and remained a popular choice of architects throughout the 20th century.

The ensuing debate on the role of computers in architecture came as no surprise.

10.4   Sunlight Simulation Studies, Dockland Square Garden, London
Carrie Byles for Skidmore Owings and Merrill 1991

10.5   Retractable Structure for Winter Garden, Paris
Nabil Gholam, Scott Dimit for Ricardo Bofill 1993

Many architects showed concern and dislike of the use of computer methods in design (Brewster 2000). However some architects adopted new technologies whilst still incorporating traditional techniques. Since the early 1990s **Nabil Gholam** (b 1962) has continuously experimented with a variety of techniques, both computer and hand combined, to express the intentions of his work. For the Winter Garden project Gholam used mixed rendering achieved with a wireframe printout from Catia software, retouched by hand with photo cutouts and Zipatone greys.

As architects recognized the benefits computer-aided design could offer, more applications of its use emerged. The analysis of urban areas, including those of significant historic importance, resulted in the creation of many CAD based presentations. In 1991 CASA, the Centre for Advanced Studies in Architecture, University of Bath, received a grant from J Sainsbury Plc to construct a 3D computer model of Bath (Day 1993). The historic parts of Glasgow and Edinburgh were also modelled on computer. The Architectural and Building Aids Computer Unit of Strathclyde (ABACUS) reported that the model of Edinburgh's old town offered a real life perspective of the visual impact of planned developments on this important part of Edinburgh (Hayward 1993). In addition, research conducted by the Alberti group of Edinburgh resulted in their development of a computer model of Edinburgh's new town. **Cesar Pelli** (b 1926) **& Associates** presented the citizens of Bilbao with several computer models and images of his plans to revitalize the area of Abandoibarra, resulting in enthusiastic participation by the people. These and many other case studies confirmed that computer simulations could help clients and lay people understand and make decisions regarding the projects being considered.

YRM were appointed in 1991 to design a replacement building for 113–117 Princes Street and 1–7 Castle Street, Edinburgh, following a fire in June 1991 which destroyed the former Palace Hotel on Princes Street and its neighbouring building on Castle Street. The fire and the demolitions that followed completely destroyed both structures down to basement level. The new buildings, within a nationally important conservation area, were to fill in the current 'gap site' in the long Princes Street elevation that looks onto Edinburgh Castle. YRM created a 3D model using Microstation, visualized in Intergraph ModelView and rendered on four 486 computers with 16mb of RAM. It won the Intergraph EuroGUG Magic Mouse Concept Visualization Award in 1993, a competition open to all European Intergraph users aimed at recognizing excellence in all aspects of computer graphic design. The perspective of the model was matched with that of the photograph of Castle Street to provide a good impression of the building in context.

10.6   Day and Night Studies of Royal Crescent Hotel, Bath
Centre for Advanced Studies in Architecture 1995

10.7   Buildings in Context, Castle Street, Edinburgh
Graham Cook for YRM 1993

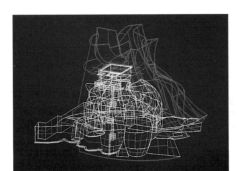

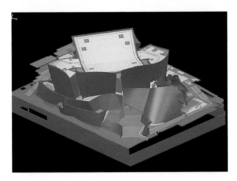

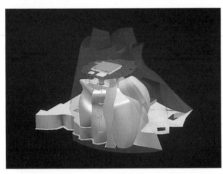

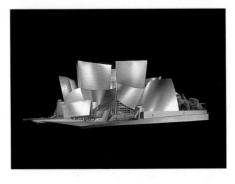

10.8   CATIA Models and Final Design Model of Walt Disney Concert Hall, Los Angeles
Frank O Gehry & Associates 1999

Many architects began to use computer-aided design through necessity rather than preference. Its application as a drafting tool became associated with improved productivity, and corporate clients, attracted by features demonstrated at trade exhibitions, began to expect computer-generated presentations. However some architects became interested in the computer first and foremost as a design tool rather than a presentation tool.

Frank Gehry (b 1929) established his first practice, **Frank O Gehry & Associates**, in 1962. The use of computer based methods became an integral part of his design practice, but CAD was not chosen for the purpose of visual presentation to clients. The practice had an established tradition of developing designs by building a series of physical models (often up to 100 or more for any given project). After the design of the Walt Disney Concert Hall was determined, via many discussions between Frank Gehry, an acoustician and several members of the orchestra, Frank Gehry began to design the exterior of the building by making models in paper with irregular, flower-like curves. The design model was then digitized using an optical digitizing system and the resulting x,y,z co-ordinates were fed into an IBM RISC 6000 computer running CATIA software. The surfaces were then rationalized in CATIA to achieve repetition without sacrificing form. A physical model was generated directly from the CATIA database, compared to the original paper model for accuracy, and the CATIA database was adjusted as necessary. The resultant 3D-computer model, containing all geometric data associated with the project, was then used as a central project database. Computer controlled fabrication and positioning machinery was driven from this model, and two dimensional documentation was exported from the model to support traditionally required documentation.

The practice never made a computer model solely for the purposes of presentation. Computer models were made only for the purpose of rationalizing the construction of complex forms. During construction of the Guggenheim Museum Bilbao a video was commissioned by Guggenheim Museum Bilbao Foundation. The video included footage of the building under construction, still images from the CATIA model and a computer simulation of the final building. This video, completed well into the construction process, was not commissioned specifically to present the design to the people of Bilbao, but rather to document the design and construction process.

Towards the end of the 20th century, Frank O Gehry & Associates were developing video conferencing and application sharing technologies to improve the co-ordination with clients and to bring them closer to the design process. The real time video of physical models, computer models and drawings were shared with clients during video conferencing sessions. The practice's use of hardware included Xi workstations and IBM RISC 6000. They adopted a Windows operating system and used AutoCAD Release 14 for 2D drawing, CATIA v4.20r1 and Rhino 1.0/1.1 for 3D modelling and Adobe Photoshop 5.5 and Paintshop Pro 5 for image editing.

In 1993 most architects were still using computer-aided design software primarily for 2D draughting. Although they appreciated 3D modelling capabilities they often lacked the time to develop new skills whilst working to tight deadlines on existing projects. However some larger practices were taking an increased interest in 3D modelling, which became increasingly useful in the search for alternative solutions to design problems. The increasingly reliable Boolean and Spline curve operations in software enabled the creation of complex geometry. Asymmetrical, organic forms began to appear which deviated from the traditional straight line and the right angle.

David Kirkland, in a press release from **Nicholas Grimshaw & Partners**, wrote *Architecture is first and foremost a three-dimensional subject, one where tactile qualities are important. Over the last 100 years, the hands-on craft of architecture has taken a backseat role to one of intellect and analysis. The architect's trained mind is always able to assimilate and study space and objects three-dimensionally; however, communicating these thoughts to non-trained people has always been of concern.* A proposal for the Waterloo roof structure was made as an initial sketch to derive a suitable solution for the project. At the time, studies of different options were being undertaken with the engineers and revolved around 2D sketches. As more information was coming to light about the constraints involved, a solution was necessary that could study these aspects together. The 3D model, produced with Integraph, provided a solution to many issues that were not solely aesthetic. Structural validity, fabrication, transportation, erection as well as aesthetics were all matters that the model was able to provide an insight into. By satisfying these aspects an elegant and workable solution was derived that could

easily be communicated to the other team members as well as the client. In 1994 the project was awarded the RIBA President's Award: Building of the Year.

The introduction of the Microsoft Windows operating system resulted in updated versions of CAD software being introduced in the early 1990s to take advantage of the features Windows offered. Windows improved ease of use, data exchange capabilities and standardization. CAD applications could be run simultaneously with image editing programs to create more artistic presentations. However issues of hardware upgrades, system optimization and staff training accompanied the improvements Windows brought. Early computer-aided design products for the Windows operating system were often simply extensions of the DOS products, and performance was slow. Applications developed specifically for the Windows environment were much faster. However the constant relearning of both CAD and Windows skills slowed the integration of CAD into working practice. Experienced architects were reluctant to learn new skills and relied on younger architects to develop the use of computers in practice. In 1993 a powerful computer system was a 486 computer, 66mhz, with 32mb RAM and 1GB hard drive. The creation of large image files necessitated good file organization when transferring files from modelling to rendering software. Several computers networked together to harness maximum power became known as *rendering farms* and were used to produce high quality renderings for presentation. Printing could involve the transfer of large files to specialist companies offering printing services, and media for data transfer ranged from fax machines, removable cartridges and optical drives to multiple floppy diskettes. The method chosen depended on the frequency with which practices needed to transfer files.

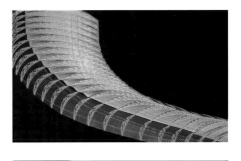

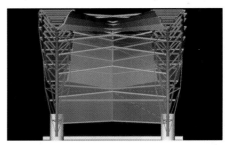
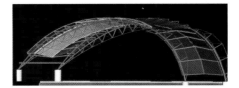

10.9 **CAD Perspectives of Waterloo International Terminal, London**
Nicholas Grimshaw & Partners 1993

The American Society of Architectural Perspectivists (ASAP) was founded in 1984 to foster communication among architectural illustrators. **John Marx** (b 1958) began to design digitally in 1992, skipping the manual drawing stage and using the computer directly. He reflected in correspondence that *the computers were considerably slower then, images may have taken 15 hours to render in 1993, where as in 1999 it would take 5 to 10 minutes. The process then was to render a small part to test lighting and colours, then great effort would be made to render overnight, when 15 hours of downtime could be found. We would also use test renderings to approximate the amount of time it would take to do the Hi Resolution rendering. This produced fewer images for final presentations, and the design study renderings back then were rather crude from a visual standpoint.* Whilst Senior Project Designer at **DES Architects and Engineers** he used CAD for the design presentation for the Oral-B Headquarters. Oral-B's goal was to create a headquarters facility that had a look and feel in keeping with a pharmaceutical image, i.e. clean and light. The architects on this project used Macintosh computers with Form Z, a 3D modelling and rendering application initially designed for architects. In the mid 1990s Form Z was primarily adopted by schools of architecture rather than by practising architects but this trend was to change in future years. John Marx had been using photographic montage with Form Z and Photoshop since 1992. The final presentation poster for Oral-B was quite innovative for its time and demonstrated that several viewpoints of a space could be experienced simultaneously in a 2D format (Architectural Record June 1994). Marx commented in discussion *The computer makes this easier to do. We would have shown our client a flat elevation, if the computer was not available as an alternative technology. This image is a vast improvement over a simple elevation.*

The mid-1990s witnessed a fast growth in the Windows market along with development of improved hardware of importance to CAD practitioners. Graphics boards, larger high-resolution monitors, scanners, digitizers and pen plotters made use of advancing technology and contributed to the growing interest in 3D modelling. Architects had increasing interest in working in 3D and had a choice of a growing number of applications (CICA 1993). Regular surveys were conducted to monitor the use of computers in architectural practice (Howes 1995, RIBA 1996, Elias and Rogers 1997).

10.10   Rendered Perspective of Oral-B Headquarters, Belmont, California
DES Architects and Engineers 1993

Many architects preferred to use the 3D modelling capabilities of computer-aided design mainly for high-quality presentations, rather than as a design tool. In 1995 **Building Design Partnership** won a national competition for the design of the Glasgow Science Centre, situated on the south side of the River Clyde. The Centre comprised three main elements, an Exhibit building, an Imax Theatre and a 100m high tower. The Glasgow office of Building Design Partnership employed approximately seventy architects, all of whom used CAD in various degrees. The relatively large size of the practice enabled opportunities for specialist skills to be developed. Some architects became specialists in three dimensional modelling and rendering using Microstation, and a smaller number specialized in animation work using 3D Studio. Conceptual design was not generally produced using 3D modelling. Many architects developed skills in image manipulation using Adobe Photoshop, which became the favourite choice for presentations used for feasibility studies and competition submissions. Multimedia software, Macromedia Director, was used for presentation purposes. Computers were causing a change in the way architects worked.

10.11   Monochrome Rendered Perspective of Glasgow Science Centre
Building Design Partnership 1995

Cesar Pelli & Associates, founded in 1977, began to use computers in 1986. Almost all the architects were trained in their use. They used the computer in early phases of the design process, producing plans, sections, elevations and renderings to present their ideas. Physical models were also used in the design process and a variety of digital media other than CAD was used for the purposes of presentation and visualization (Uddin 1999).

The National Museum of Contemporary Art, Osaka, Japan, was designed for an irregular and extremely tight site adjacent to an existing Science Museum. The museum, distributed on three levels below grade, has a first level that is the public free zone, followed by two levels of temporary and permanent gallery space. Whilst it was agreed that the entire building was built underground, the architect was requested to give the new museum a prominent and distinctive image. The entrance has thus been conceived as a sculptural form and a metal (brass) physical model of this entrance was constructed. AutoCAD was used to draw the plan of the Entry Level of Osaka, which included elliptical forms, spline curves, hatch patterns and line types. A sense of building scale was achieved by the representation of people in the rendered section of the museum. The practice used PCs running on Windows operating system and used AutoCAD, Accurender, 3D Studio, Lightscape, Photoshop, Paintshop Pro, Illustrator and QuarkXPress.

In the mid to late 1990s practices were installing computer network infrastructures. Computer-aided design software had to be *network friendly* to meet the needs of changing working practices.

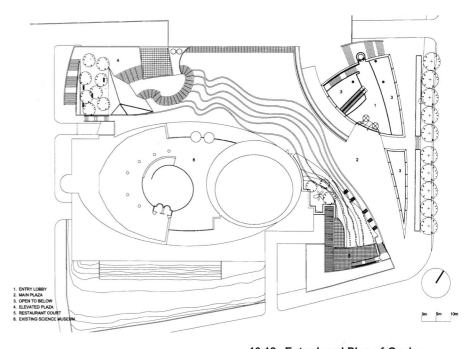

1. ENTRY LOBBY
2. MAIN PLAZA
3. OPEN TO BELOW
4. ELEVATED PLAZA
5. RESTAURANT COURT
6. EXISTING SCIENCE MUSEUM

0m   5m   10m

10.12   Entry Level Plan of Osaka Museum, Japan
Cesar Pelli & Associates 1996

10.13   Rendered Section of Osaka Museum, Japan
Cesar Pelli & Associates 1996

Towards the end of the twentieth century available software allowed for greater exploration of materials, texture, colour and lighting in design. The trend for high quality presentations increased, with concern for improved atmosphere, colour manipulation, scale and lighting effects.

10.14 Gift Shop, London
Ayssar Arida for Nabil Gholam 1999

10.15 Xscape™ Castleford Indoor Ski Slope, Pontefract
Andrew Hilton for FaulknerBrowns 1999

10.16 Toshiba House, Frimley, Surrey
Derek Lovejoy Partnership with GMW 1999

FaulknerBrowns produced the rendered night-time perspective of Xscape™ Castleford indoor ski slope with 3D Studio. The sleek aero-dynamic form, detailed foreground and interesting lighting effects combined to create an atmospheric quality to the presentation.

Derek Lovejoy (1925–2000) **Partnership** used computer-aided design after 1990, using in-house software as well as industry standard programs. The rendered perspective of Toshiba House demonstrated great attention to ground and landscape texture.

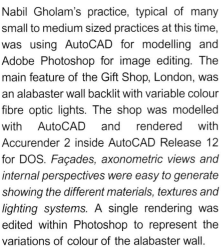

Nabil Gholam's practice, typical of many small to medium sized practices at this time, was using AutoCAD for modelling and Adobe Photoshop for image editing. The main feature of the Gift Shop, London, was an alabaster wall backlit with variable colour fibre optic lights. The shop was modelled with AutoCAD and rendered with Accurender 2 inside AutoCAD Release 12 for DOS. *Façades, axonometric views and internal perspectives were easy to generate showing the different materials, textures and lighting systems.* A single rendering was edited within Photoshop to represent the variations of colour of the alabaster wall.

Towards the end of the 20th century more informal compositions emerged. 'Digital collages' were composed of computer-generated plans and elevations with rendered perspective views. This technique presented ideas in more artistic terms and provided a softer presentation than the harsh lines of some computer generated images. In 1999 **Form 4 Architects** did 80 per cent of their work on computers, and demonstrated how small architectural practices (they employed 13 people) could handle projects often considered beyond the scope of small firms (Novitski February 2000). The practice used FormZ for 3D modelling and design, Adobe Photoshop for image editing and QuarkXPress for desktop publishing. John Marx, in current discussion, commented on the techniques used: *We thought we would create some posters that would describe the essence of the project, both for the client as well as the public. We started by selecting specific views of the project which expressed some of the compositional and conceptual relationships both between buildings, and in the form of the buildings. The long horizontal format of the posters reflected the sleek horizontal nature of the architecture.*

10.17   San Tomas R&D Campus, Santa Clara, California
Form 4 Architects 1999

The image of the building was rendered at high resolution after some fine-tuning of the lighting requirements. The background cloud was added using Photoshop. The building image and cloud were placed onto a black background, black chosen to blend all the elements together, and provide a dramatic effect through contrast. Some wireframe images of the project were overlaid behind the rendered images. Each image, including the clouds, was placed on different layers in Photoshop then scrutinized for levels of transparency. Many of the layers had *layer masks* applied, allowing the image to translucently fade across a background. This created textural richness, and a sense of balance between the elements. John Marx observed that *such digital collages have become feasible through greater speeds of computer processing which significantly reduce rendering time. Photorealistic images can be produced for very early design studies, and final renderings can have greater detail in the model geometry, more texture maps at larger sizes, and raytraced shadows and reflections without concern. The extra time has enabled experimentation with more unusual rendering techniques, including collages.*

Two project presentations by **Ian Ritchie** (b 1947) **Architects** demonstrated the maturing of computer-aided design presentations. Emphasis on atmospheric quality, colour depth and balance, and high resolution conveyed a uniqueness of style and illustrated how computer-aided design and other graphic techniques were overlapping. Architects were applying digital media in a variety of forms and digital photomontages were playing an important part in presentation.

The influence of schools of architecture with regard to computer technology was summarized by Uddin (1999): *Practitioners in the 1980s have blamed architecture schools for not preparing new graduates for the new technology, especially CAD. That trend has changed during the 1990s. Now fresh graduates bring more diverse and comprehensive computer knowledge than ever before.*

10.18 Magna Carta Visitor Centre, Salisbury Cathedral
Ian Ritchie Architects 1999

10.19 Alba di Milano, Italy
Ian Ritchie Architects 1999

Richard Rogers Partnership used a combination of traditional and digital techniques, applied *as appropriate* to the design process.

Towards the end of the 20th century the studio operated within a mobile 'hot desking' environment where every workstation had the availability of a wide choice of software from desktop publishing to computer-aided design and 3D rendering. All architectural staff were trained in a variety of application and process driven digital techniques allowing them to make both the decisions on, and use of, the appropriate technology.

Prior to 1999 the practice used a Macintosh platform, post January 1999 Windows. Software used includes MicroStation, AutoCAD, Illustrator, Freehand, 3D Studio, Form Z, Lightscape, Photoshop, Adobe Premier, QuarkXPress, Indesign, Adobe Acrobat, Powerpoint and Director. Software was selected for its appropriateness of use for concept designs, 2D drawings, 3D models, image manipulation, desktop publishing and Virtual Reality and animation.

10.20   3D Rendering, Antwerp Court House, Antwerpen
Richard Rogers Partnership 1999

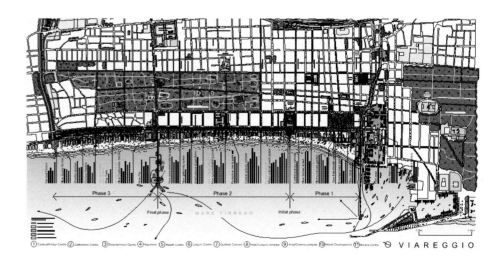

10.21   2D Drawing, Viareggio, Italy
Richard Rogers Partnership 1999

One of **Norman Foster and Partners'** earliest projects using computer-aided design was London's third airport, Stanstead, in 1981. In 1995 the practice won the CICA 3D Merit award for Holborn Place office project, drawn with MicroStation. The practice continued to present their ideas to clients through the use of photomontage, placing buildings in context. Rendered daytime and night-time views enabled design teams to assess design proposals and to further develop their ideas.

10.22 Photomontage, Gateshead Music Centre, Gateshead
Foster and Partners 1999

Throughout the 1990s many architects preferred to commission specialist illustrators to do their visualizations for them. In America, Williams (2000) described how an architectural illustrator, Ernest Burden, took a hybrid approach to visualization. Burden used a combination of digital images together with traditional drawing and painting techniques to make presentations as artistic as possible. He used software application DataCAD, which supported his hybrid approach to rendering.

Hayes Davidson, set up in 1989 by Alan Davidson, had become leading computer illustrators in the UK, and had an impressive client list of leading architects. Davidson, who had a long association with the CICA CAD awards, both in winning awards and latterly judging the competition, firmly believed that no amount of advanced technology could represent buildings successfully without an illustrator with an artistic eye. The practice employed staff who first and foremost had an eye for illustration, and secondly had an aptitude for computing. Their work was done using various PCs and operating systems, using software applications favoured by individual team people: AutoCAD, 3D Studio and Form Z for 3D modelling, Photoshop for image editing, Electric Image, Premiere, Flash and QuickTime VR for animations.

10.23 No. 1 Poultry, London
Hayes Davidson for James Stirling
Michael Wilford and Associates 1998

Hayes Davidson created a series of images for a design by Richard Rogers Partnership for the Saitama Arena in Japan. A night time study of the stadium won the Building Design Award in the 1996 CICA CAD Drawing Awards, renamed the CICA Computer Graphics Awards in 1997 to reflect the changing nature of computer visualizations. Lyall (1997) described the quality of the images produced by Hayes Davidson as stunningly persuasive, and the RIBA drawing collection was extended to include their work in video format.

10.24   Saitama Arena, Japan
Hayes Davidson for Richard Rogers
Partnership 1995

The early days of the CICA CAD Awards produced some attractive colour perspectives, although Jill Lever, Curator of the RIBA Drawings Collection at that time, believed that colour was generally used with too little restraint (CICA 1989). As the years progressed, illustrators became more skilled in assessing the appropriate level of detail required for effective presentations, and the use of computer-aided design became more sophisticated. Architectural practice sought to produce computer-generated *photo-realistic* images, and clients were expecting these as normal practice. The use of 3D modelling was increasing.

At the beginning of the 21st century architects were becoming increasingly dependent on computers, although smaller practices were generally less dependent than larger firms (CICA 2000). Whilst acknowledging the preciseness that CAD could bring to images, some architectural researchers and practices were searching for ways to bring art and expression back into computer-generated illustrations. The computer industry, responding to this requirement, continued to develop intuitive image manipulation and paintbox software, and specialist visualization packages.

11.0   Retail Development Salford
MUSE Virtual Presence for
J Sainsbury plc 1993

Virtual Reality (VR) is the name of an interactive computer technology that attempts to create a completely convincing illusion of being immersed in an artificial world that exists only inside a computer (Rheingold 1991). Virtual Reality adds the dimension of animation to computer models. The history of VR can be traced back to the early 1950s, although most of the key developments occurred in the USA in the 1980s (Stone 1994). Stone noted that it was late in 1990 that VR came to the public's attention in Britain when work by researchers was presented at a London Computer Graphics Conference. Previously research into visualization and computer animation had been concerned with rendering and geometric modelling.

In a bibliography on computer animation Thalmann and Thalmann (1992) noted that from the first paper by Ken Knowlton in 1964, evolution of computer animation had been spectacular. Computer systems, which allow ordinary users to explore simulated spaces in real time, had long been a goal in the computer graphics community (Miller *et al*. 1992). Many VR systems became commercially available.

The potential for Virtual Reality technology was recognized by many disciplines and applications developed in the fields of aeronautics, engineering, communications, psychology, education and medicine (Dupont 1994). The Virtual Reality Society was formed in 1994 to provide a discussion forum for VR related issues.

As most of the advances in this technology came about only in the 1980s and 1990s the technology was regarded as relatively new, still changing and maturing (Jayaram 1997). It was perceived by many as being in its infancy (Manisty 1997), requiring expensive hardware and video devices, and being mainly appropriate for the games market. In 1994 an initiative was launched in the UK to help companies assess the potential of Virtual Reality without investing in expensive and easily outdated computer hardware and software (Stone 1994). Types of Virtual Reality included sensory immersion (headsets, gloves etc.), simulator VR (flights etc.), desktop VR and Virtual Reality Centres (small cinema-like studios). The increasing power of the PC and growing number of VR applications resulted in a growth in desktop VR, which offered businesses a cost-effective way to make use of the technology.

In 1993 one of the UK's major food retailers, Sainsbury's, produced a requirement for a virtual supermarket. The company believed that Virtual Reality technology had potential to contribute to the design process. The project offered a practical evaluation of the Virtual Reality technologies available at that time. Plans and drawings of an existing store enabled interior and exterior layouts of a virtual store to be developed using PC and Unix workstation Virtual Reality software. The visualizations were produced by Virtual Presence, a computer graphics company with a history going back to 1989. Virtual Presence designed a system named ConceptVR, a Virtual Reality space planning system that could run on accelerated PCs. The company offered a service to many fields, including architecture, that were beginning to take an interest in VR.

The Centre for Advanced Studies in Architecture (CASA), University of Bath, also created an animation of a proposal by Sainsbury's for the city of Bath in 1993. The Bath Model grew to include a model of the Southgate Centre, produced for a public exhibition/consultation exercise in 1998. Towards the end of 1999 CASA produced computer animations for the John Soane exhibition at the Royal Academy, London.

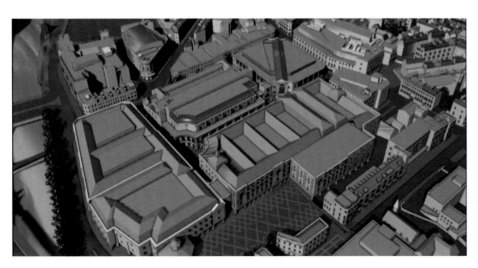

11.1   Southgate Centre, Bath
CASA for Chapman Taylor 1998

The need for specialists in visualization continued. Insite Environments, a landscape architectural practice set up in 1992, offered visualization services to practising architects, planners and developers. Illustrators developed VR models for environmental assessment and urban and landscape design. They found that planning supported by Virtual Reality resulted in reduced cost of inquiries. The practice emphasized the importance of preciseness and accuracy in computer modelling, especially if it were to be used as part of a public inquiry. They made use of a range of software including Superscape Visualizer, 3D Studio, Macromedia Director, and Quicktime VR. Insite found that clients generally favoured the animation provided by 3D Studio, which, although non-interactive, could model materials, texture and lighting to create realistic scenes. However while VR software offering an interactive environment was compromised on the level of material detailing, primarily because of the limitations of PC processing power available at the time, it did offer more potential in negotiating planning consent. In any event a simpler amount of detail was usually appropriate to discuss design issues. Speed of real-time rendering, the cost of effective output devices and rather plain landscapes were concerns that lessened towards the end of the 20th century. The Pudding Chare VR project was a simple massing study to examine appropriate scale for new apartments proposed alongside a listed building. It helped with proposals for the demolition of a neighbouring building.

**11.2   Pudding Chare Massing Study,
Newcastle upon Tyne**
Insite Environments for Miller Homes
1997

The potential contribution of Virtual Reality for assessment of design implications of projects prior to commencement was recognized in the UK by Sir Michael Latham (1994) who stated: *It is rarely satisfactory for clients to be shown conceptual drawings, still less outline plans of rooms. The design team must offer the client a vision of the project in a form which it can understand and change in time.* Developers and researchers world-wide recognized the growing need for easy-to-use design tools to enable the exploration of options early in the design process.

At Eindhoven University of Technology in the Netherlands a research program called VR-DIS concentrated on the application of computers in architectural design. This involved a wide range of research topics, varying from research on computer-aided design methods, information and process modelling, to the use of Virtual Reality as a new medium in architectural design. Researchers at Eindhoven developed DDDoolz, a system for mass study and spatial design in the early conceptual stage of the design process. The system produced models that the user could slowly rotate, walk through or fly over while drawing or editing. Sketching with DDDoolz was described to be like painting blocks in space. Although simple 3D models were preferred in early design, once a design option was agreed the model could be enhanced in image editing software such as Photoshop or imported into 3D Studio. With visual quality improved further possible scenarios on materials, textures and lighting could be explored.

Bauke de Vries (b 1957) of the Design Systems Group, Eindhoven University of Technology, commented: *Sketching in 3D seems to be a paradox. The sketch activity is inherently 2D since it is executed in a plane on a flat surface using some drawing device (e.g. a pencil). Three dimensional creation and manipulation of objects presumes the activity being executed in a 3D environment on spatial objects. Nevertheless, sketching in 3D represents a design activity that plays a very important role in the architectural design process and it has attracted many researchers ever since the Electronic Sketchpad of Ivan Sutherland.*

The development of new computer systems to support the creation of 3D forms by means of 3D sketching was seen by some as a fundamental step in transforming the computer from a tool into a new medium for design (Asanowicz 1999). Not everyone shared this view and the debate relating to computer based sketching continued.

Practitioners who used computers for simple 3D modelling early in design accepted commercially available software such as ArchiCAD, Design Workshop, Form Z, VectorWorks, Microstation Triforma and DataCAD as effective tools. ArchiCAD was one of the few architecture-focused programs that remained available for both PC and Macintosh platforms. The architectural profession demonstrated a loyalty to Macintosh throughout the 20th century, citing the issue of *ease of use* as a key contributing factor.

11.3   DDDoolz model
Bauke de Vries for Eindhoven University of Technology 1999

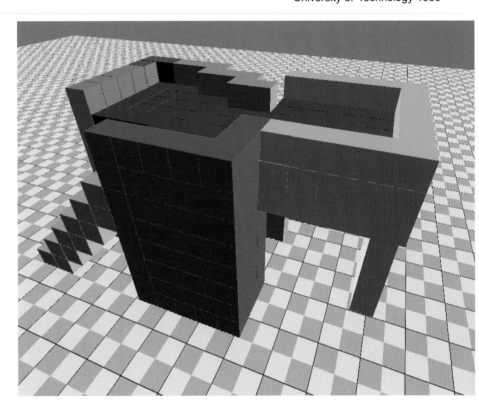

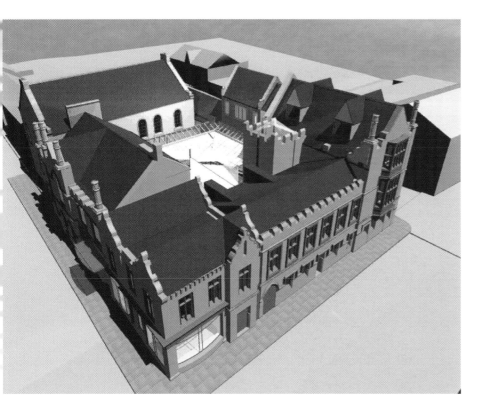

Throughout the 1990s a type of animation that attracted much attention was the architectural walk-through. This technique involved building scenes using geometric objects and enabling users to navigate between the objects. This simulated the effect of walking around a building or area and experiencing the *feel* of the environment. Architects and illustrators built on their knowledge of CAD and 3D modelling to add animation into presentations, initially in a non-immersive way, viewing the artificial world from the outside.

The images of Old Town Hall, exterior and interior, were taken from an animation which explored how a listed building was to be converted into business starter units, a café and auditorium. The animation, produced using 3D Studio Max, simulated textures and the reflective quality of steel, glass and stone, but the interactivity of Virtual Reality was unavailable, making this type of presentation more appropriate for marketing than planning purposes.

The transfer of computer animations to video tape, for project presentation, was far from a simple process (Boesjes 1993). In the mid-1990s a 540mb hard disk would store around three minutes of video. Specialist bureaux set up to offer video-animation services to architects. However as technology developed and prices reduced, it became possible for architects to create computer-video animations within their practice (Bartlett 1996).

11.4   Old Town Hall, North Shields
Insite Environments for North
Tyneside Challenge 1999

The sequencing of images to represent movement enabled fly-overs as well as walk-throughs to be produced. Clients could be presented with aerial views of project proposals.

Nabil Gholam inserted a computer rendering, produced in SoftImage, of a large-scale urban project into an aerial view of the site. An animation was created to *fly over* the marina. This use of a photomontage, placing the marina in context, helped the client and town planners to envision the project and address any issues of concern.

Despite the possibilities that walk-through and fly-over animations created, if a presentation lacked interaction then clients were still performing the role of a spectator, rather than having the illusion of *being there*. However the potential of the early Virtual Reality systems to develop into tools for intuitive, interactive and realistic evaluation of future environments was recognized (Achten *et al.* 1999). This potential, and speed of progress in technological developments, led to the term *cyberspace* being linked to architecture (Toy 1998).

As with CAD, widespread use of Virtual Reality would follow the availability of appropriate commercial software systems. Division, a Virtual Reality software company, made significant contributions in this field throughout the 1990s. Division provided a full range of visualization software to enable interaction in a virtual environment. Capabilities such as interactive flying and associativity with CAD data became available in 2000.

Superscape also was a product that brought the world of Virtual Reality to the desktop of architectural practices. Software that could operate on a PC, rather than expensive Unix workstations, helped the integration of VR into the architectural work environment (*Virtual Reality World* Nov/Dec 1994).

11.5 Joseph Khoury Marina, Beirut
AXYZ 3D consultants for Nabil Gholam 1997

A technique that proved interesting to architectural practice was one that allowed interaction with photographic images. The method involved taking a 360-degree photomontage and mapping it to the interior of an imaginary sphere. Combinations of photographs and 3D models could be used and the view of a person standing inside the sphere resulted in a display of a real or virtual environment. Many interesting examples of this form of presentation emerged as architects discovered its ability to produce animations. The Apple® QuickTime® system became established in this area and allowed the creation of three dimensional virtual worlds and interactive presentations on Macintosh computers (Uddin 1999). Surround Video software was the PC alternative.

Richard Rogers Partnership used Apple® QuickTime® VR Authoring Studio to create an interactive animation of Terminal Five, Heathrow Airport, Middlesex. This presentation was based on a 3D computer model of Terminal 5 with images from the model tiled together as if mapped to the interior of a sphere. The resultant 360° panorama enabled different areas of the airport to be visualized.

The creation of computer animations, interactive or non-interactive, generated large file sizes, and questions arose about the most appropriate media for transferring such files for purposes of project presentation. Output to compact disc or video format aided portability between locations, but the development of the Internet and World Wide Web greatly assisted in this area. The Internet initially grew out of an American research project that investigated how to exchange files between remote computers via long-distance telephone lines. Its development and rapid growth became well-documented (Bridges 1996) and the potential of the Internet and World Wide Web (WWW), appreciated initially by researchers and educators, became recognized by commerce. It subsequently developed into a vast network which achieved remarkable growth from the mid 1990s onwards.

Architectural practices, large and small, recognized the importance of the WWW as a medium for presentation, although initially there was concern about security and speed of transfer. A significant development for the architect was that of Virtual Reality Modelling Language (VRML), a programming language for the definition of Web-based 3D worlds. Software was developed specifically to model and display VRML worlds. The language could also be integrated with many popular CAD programs, particularly if the CAD models had been created with Virtual Reality in mind. Web browsers were developed and provided familiar interfaces for viewing VRML worlds, which offered reduced file size and speed improvements via real time interaction. In 1996 Microsoft incorporated Supercape's Viscape as part of the Internet Explorer Starter Kit. 3D virtual worlds could be viewed and accessed regardless of location.

At the beginning of the 21st century architects increasingly used WWW technology to display their projects. By accessing an architect's web site it became possible for clients to view ideas from architects' offices regardless of distance between them. Video and computer animations particular benefited by this media which enabled project collaboration in a way not possible before.

11.6   Heathrow Airport Terminal 5, London
Richard Rogers Partnership 1995

Presentations became increasingly composed of a variety of media: scanned or rendered still images, text, computer animations, video and sound. The Construction Industry Computing Association (CICA) was recognizing the multimedia nature of many architectural presentations. Hayes Davidson, who had won CICA awards for three successive years, 1994 to 1996, worked with **Arup Associates** on the design for the City of Manchester Stadium and created a series of digital images for the project. Hayes Davidson enthusiastically embraced technological developments to incorporate animation and interactivity into their work. They extended their services to include web design and created sites for leading architects. The company developed the first digital interactive 3D-computer representation of London in 1997. The project, entitled London eCity, incorporated 3D computer models, Virtual Reality, aerial and satellite photography, 2D images, maps of London, text and video. The resultant interactive presentation was shown at the opening of the Architecture Foundation's 'New London Architecture' exhibition held in November 1997.

11.7   City of Manchester Stadium
Hayes Davidson for Arup Associates
1998

London eCity and other simulations of city centres throughout the world developed from their initial inception and encouraged debate on both proposed and historic developments (AlSayyad 1996, Holmgren and Rüdiger 1999).

A major retrospective exhibition of the work of **Foster and Partners** was staged in 2000 at the Sainsbury Centre for Visual Arts, University of East Anglia, Norwich. The exhibition, 'Exploring The City', featured many of Foster's landmark projects and buildings and included interactive computer displays, video, film and slide projections as well as traditional artwork. The Greater London Authority Assembly Building was one of the practice's current projects on display. The exhibition was sponsored by Bentley Systems, the company whose software had been adopted by Foster and Partners for presentation and design purposes.

The use of computer modelling and animation proved useful in Foster's proposals for the design of the Bilbao Metro. *Foster's idea of the treatment of the interior as a cavern was initially not well received. But a computer model showing a virtual journey dissipated all doubts and showed the luminosity and space sensation of the cavern* (Sanchez 1999). The presentation contained not only the geometry of the design, but also the idea behind it.

**11.8   Greater London Authority
Assembly Headquarters**
Foster and Partners 1999

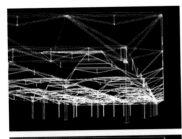

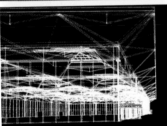

New computing languages and design environments were providing architects with interesting alternatives to the limitations of computer-aided design systems and graphical presentation methods of the past (Romero 1998). **YRM** was commissioned to design a new terminal, including interior design, for Bristol International Airport. CAD was used extensively in the design, from the production of initial wireframe models up to high quality renderings, presented as still images. The increased performance of computer systems allowed the rendering of multiple images to produce walk-through animations. The use of Virtual Reality at YRM increased to form a major part of the design process. It was used to communicate design solutions to the client and other members of the project team from early feasibility stages onwards. YRM believed that the use of VR technology greatly enhanced client understanding. The practice adopted a Windows NT system, and all technical staff had access to CAD software MicroStation J/Triforma. VR animation was transferred to the medium of a compact disc or video or placed on their web site for subsequent viewing. YRM prepared 3D computer panoramic views of the spaces within the landside and airside lounges in the Terminal at Bristol International Airport. The panoramic views enabled assessment of sight lines, visibility and proposed layout and were used as an integral part of the consultation process with all the people involved.

11.9   Bristol International Airport, Stages of Development
Graham Cook for YRM 1999

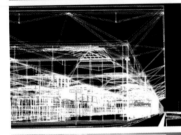

11.10   Bristol International Airport, VR Panorama
YRM 1999

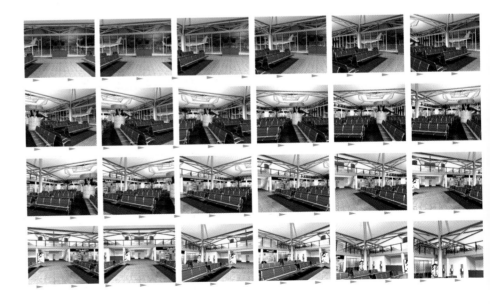

Images of a proposed virtual library were produced for the ACADIA 1999 design competition *Library for the Information Age*. The chair-like element represented the proposed physical artefact to be used as an interface. Other images represented the virtual world in which the information would be searched and retrieved.

The images were from an excellent archive of students' work from the Imaging Laboratory of the School of Architecture, New Jersey Institute of Technology. Architect, instructor and design critic **Glenn Goldman** (b 1952) and **Steve Zdepski** (b 1946) were the first in the US to create fully electronic architectural design studios and had taught digital design continuously since 1985. Their approach was quite innovative for the 1980s in that they produced a 3D model first, and from this derived the more traditional 2D views.

Their earliest project and first attempt at 3D modelling was created with MegaMODEL and shaded with MegaSHADE – both by MegaCADD Corporation running on IBM-AT (6Mhz) machines (Architectural Record January 1988).

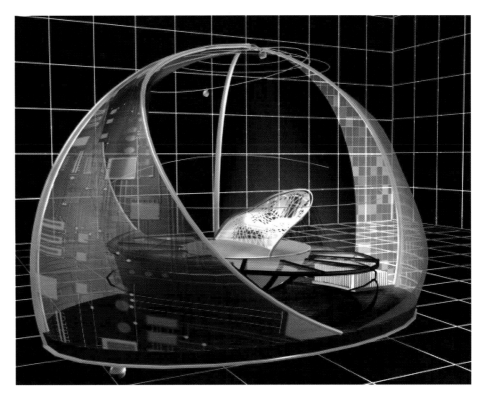

11.11 Library for the Information Age
Mariko Fujitsuka for School of Architecture, New Jersey Institute of Technology 1999

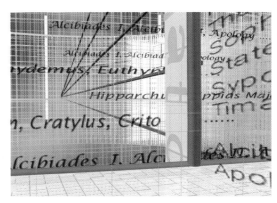

Virtual Reality technology matured throughout the 1990s. Interactive, 3D worlds were being used in an increasing number of fields. Whilst the impact of Virtual Reality and other digital techniques on architectural practice could not be ignored, surveys to investigate how architectural practitioners were using computers revealed that animated presentations were still used relatively infrequently (Conlon 2000, Szalapaj and Chang 1999, Fallon 1998). Despite initiatives such as the UK Virtual Reality Forum, set up to promote the commercial use of Virtual Reality in the UK, the majority of computer assisted architectural presentations were comprised of rendered still images.

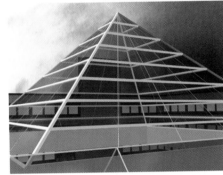

11.12 Manchester Business School
MUSE Virtual Presence for
University of Manchester 2000

Nonetheless, presentations were becoming more seductive and the architect's relationship with the client improved with the ability to communicate information more effectively and frequently. Specialist illustrators and architectural practices adopting VR technology were demonstrating how art, design and technology could be combined to achieve a client's brief. Manchester Business School commissioned the creation of a simple but flexible virtual environment to enable university staff, designers, architects and students to discuss, refine and approve the development of the School's inner quadrangle. Large screen projection displays were used for presentation purposes. The model, developed by Virtual Presence, was to be further developed to present more detailed architectural design. Virtual Presence demonstrated that computer-aided design and Virtual Reality were complimentary technologies, and that integration problems were minimized if the CAD model was created with the real-time interactive demands of VR in mind.

At the end of the 20th century architects were offered lessons on the creation of artificial worlds by a rapidly developing computer games industry (Richens and Trinder 1999, Knight and Brown 1999). The Martin Centre for Architectural and Urban Studies, University of Cambridge, set out to adapt games software to build an internet-deliverable VR experience of a new computer laboratory designed by architects RMJM for the university. Although the value of entertainment software to architects was not new (Battle and McCarthy 1994), companies world-wide were recognizing how games software, such as Unreal from GT Interactive, and other WWW resources could contribute to the creation of artificial 3D worlds.

Educators also acknowledged that the entertainment industry offered lessons to architects, and additionally recognized that architects themselves could help in the creation of artificial worlds for entertainment. Students of architecture at the New Jersey Institute of Technology designed sets for sequels to, or remakes of, various films. Samantha Hockins designed a proposed set for a sequel to the motion picture *March of the Wooden Soldiers*. The project was created with 3D Studio MAX and then processed with Adobe Photoshop.

Goldman (2000) comments in correspondence *What is interesting, I think, in the context of artists' impressions in architectural design, is that architectural education has expanded to include – at least at an introductory level – set design, game design, and web design as well as traditional building design. The scope of what architecture students see as part of architectural design has expanded. To be sure, we still deal with buildings, structure, lighting, acoustics, and so on – but digital media have allowed us to do much more. The lines between art, architecture, and entertainment have been blurred.*

11.13 Set for Motion Picture
Samantha Hockins for School of Architecture, New Jersey Institute of Technology 1999

At the end of the 20th century the fields of architecture and Virtual Reality were becoming intertwined. Virtual Reality added another technique to the rich history of architectural representation. VR technology demonstrated potential to aid the process of architectural design and to provide virtual worlds that could support project collaboration. The role of architectural design itself in the creation of these virtual environments was beginning to be addressed (Bridges 2000). Educators world-wide were recognizing the potential of computers to create virtual environments. Talented new graduates entered architectural practice increasingly computer literate and more able to integrate VR into the architectural working environment. Experienced architects of an older generation, who had been resisting the use of VR as a design tool, could not ignore its potential for the exploration and presentation of architectural designs.

As the price of technology decreases Virtual Reality will become more common. Software will describe the look, sound and feel of an artificial world, down to the smallest detail. (Gates 1996)

12.0   Virtual Artificial Ecology, Interior Perspective Section
Christian Groothuizen for Bartlett School of Architecture, University College London 2000

Chapter 12 **Where Next? Ideas and Conclusions**

split site three: interior perspective section
frame 170:360   view through eversion space

The last decades of the 20th century saw architectural representation once again in the process of redefinition (Lipstadt 1989). Architectural practices had to continually evaluate the benefits of using digital technology against the costs of doing so. The demands and pressures of an increasingly commercial world, to create architecture quickly, at less cost, meant that the speed and flexibility of CAD and Virtual Reality were considered increasingly advantageous when compared with the more traditional techniques of drawing, painting and models. New technology was becoming more accessible and sophisticated, and some architects' offices were exclusively computer-based.

Whilst a growing number of practices were acknowledging the potential of the computer as a design tool, many used it predominantly as a medium for presentation. Yet could it ever make a substitute for *the empty canvas of the painter, the block of marble of the sculptor, or the blank lined sheets of the composer?* (Wright 1989). Artists debated whether the computer was simply a tool, or a medium that heralded a new art form. Architects wondered if that emotional link between the viewer and the artist's impression of a building design would ever be achievable with the new technology. As with many innovations, early computer tools were more difficult to use, and therefore experience with art took a back seat to experience with technology (Claridge 1996). A preoccupation with the tools rather than the desired product could lead to images that were technically rich but lacking in emotive quality. The Inter Society for the Electronic Arts (ISEA) was formed in 1990 to consider the creative, theoretical and technological aspects of electronic art. ISEA symposiums encourage active debate and exchange on art, technology and the new media.

Graham Morrison (Allies and Morrison) commented *artists offer a different kind of quality you just can't get from a computer simulation. You get a sense of reality whereas computers tend to produce normality.* However, in a discussion on the aesthetic issues in computer art, Nadin (1989) purported that *provided we are able to adopt a different notion of art and a different notion of artist, many arguments speak in favour of an increased interpretative approach, of more performances and larger audiences, and of aesthetic products new in their condition, impact and social implications.*

The custom for architects to employ independent artists has continued into the 21st century, not only for computer presentations but also for those using traditional media. According to David Eccles, an architectural illustrator for 30 years, *despite the computer revolution, there are plenty of illustrators and artists still being commissioned by architects who want an alternative to CAD images.* He said: *I tend to be commissioned by larger practices, very few people can draw anyway. Quite large firms come to me for relatively simple drawing that 10 years ago they would have given to the juniors. For a one-off quick image, I can do a view of a building immensely quicker than a machine* (*Building Design* 8 May 1998). Gerald Green is an architectural illustrator who works with a number of well-known architectural practices. He comments *We are absolutely not a dying breed and we're certainly not being totally replaced by computer images* (*Building Design* 8 May 1998).

The number of societies for architectural illustrators throughout the world is indeed evidence that many architects prefer not to do all of their illustrations in-house, but to commission artistic specialists to produce representations for them. Illustrators, who can offer individual and unique techniques and traditional personally crafted design work, remain in demand alongside those who have mastered the techniques of digital art.

Despite personal preferences we must question whether the end results of today's computer representations are less impressive than those representations of our ancestors. The process itself still requires the ingredients of imagination, exploration, discipline, skill, honesty, trust and artistic licence. Yet the physical forms of computer renderings and traditional artists' impressions are quite distinct and arouse different emotions. The personal intimacy of a drawing adds to our emotional feeling about it. A painting can be hung in a gallery or museum, for all to see. CAD renderings and animations will be displayed in *Virtual Museums*, themselves based on advancing technology. Those worthy enough to be included in architectural collections will be displayed via the media of computer screen, CD or video. Yet despite this difference of physical form, the use of technology need not mean a decline in artistic representation itself. The most successful computer illustrators are those with, first and foremost, an eye for art and architecture, the science of technology being a means to an end.

New technologies of today can hasten the translation of idea into material expression and can communicate design intention to larger, more widespread audiences. They herald craftsmanship of a different era.

As new skills gain more credibility and acceptance we wonder whether we shall witness a decline of traditional techniques. Sketching, drawing, painting and model making have been extended to include computer-aided design and Virtual Reality. These skills are inter-related to varying degrees, and are taught differently depending on the institution. *All students in the 21st century must be fluent in manipulating perspective projections and navigating through spatial simulations* (Clayton and Vasquez de Velasco 1999). Clayton goes on to state that *drafting is becoming formalized and automated. While instruction in the conventions of drafting will be still necessary, the mechanics of producing orthographic projections are rapidly being automated.*

Although some architects have an aptitude for computing, many still need to develop ability in computer modelling to use the computer as both a presentation and design tool. The rapid advancement of technology in the latter decades of the 20th century created a generation gap amongst architects and resulted in some detachment of the architect from computer-generated imagery. Experienced architects were not immediately computer-literate. Computer-capable architects tended to be of the younger generation, and many were employed initially to produce fashionable CAD renderings. The ideas of experienced architects were being represented by a younger generation. In the early days of computer graphics, analytical effort and logical deduction were useful in applying a technology designed more for scientific purposes. Computers did not lend themselves to *art* until increased processing power signalled improvements in the interaction between human and machine. Early application of CAD in architectural practice was in simply extending traditional design and draughting techniques. Much time was spent on learning the new technology, but

mastering it proved to take a little longer. However computers are now much more accessible to architects and artists, and greatly improved hardware and software is developed with art in mind. Imaging software, enabling a softer delineated finish to be added to the previously hard-edged computer image, is adopted widely by architects and artists alike, some of whom print non-photorealistic imagery onto artists' watercolour paper. Computer illustrators employ staff with an artistic eye, working with their preferred software, just as painters would work with their preferred paper and brushes, model-makers with their preferred material and implements.

Architects' expectations from the computer industry have grown to encompass the ideal of fully integrated design, production and presentation software (Brewster 2000). The importance of such integrated tools to enhance the skills of architects is recognized by the computer graphics research community. *Seamless, invisible computing* was predicted for the 21st century by Ray Kurzweil, keynote at SIGGRAPH's Annual Conference on Computer Graphics and Interactive Techniques (*ArchitectureWeek* August 2000). Such integration will perhaps lead to reflection once again on the ownership of representations, which is not always clear. Some traditional drawings and paintings are recognized instantly by the style of the artist. **Pugin** had a great love of drawing, and did all of his sketches, drawings, plans and details himself, resulting in the individuality of all his work (Wedgewood 1998). Other drawings and designs are more difficult to attribute. However *the digital medium is one of instant replication and perfect fidelity; therefore the notion of the original, the aura of uniqueness, and the attraction of ownership will have to undergo reinterpretation and change*

(Nadin 1989). An electronic image can be easily edited, and may be worked upon by several people. This does however offer advantages in effecting greater degrees of *interaction*, which aids both creativity and communication.

Advancing technology has increased the range of skills required of the architect. Good management skills are required for the effective use of three dimensional models, the co-ordination of data from different disciplines and the retrieval of images from large databases. Architects, concerned to preserve accuracy and improve productivity, acknowledge that shared standards and compatibility of data will effect productivity gains. Nigel Davies of Whitby Bird and Partners said *we wrote special macros to make the process of installing all configuration files a one-click exercise, reducing the likelihood of errors and the need for constant support* (*Building Design* 6 October 2000). According to Winterkorn (2000) a survey by the British Research Establishment and the CICA identified improved quality of communication as the most important benefit of information technology for architects. The survey highlighted the need for information technology to serve the needs of the profession, not the other way round. Education and training can aid the effective use of computers in practice. **Neil Spiller** (b 1961), architect, author and teacher at the Bartlett School of Architecture, University College London, believes the time has come to reassess architectural education, to enliven and diversify it to meet the needs of the 21st century (Spiller 1998).

In America, whilst the teaching of computer skills to students varies widely between institutions, some educators believe that the computer's importance is not for 2D drafting, but for creating a highly effective simulated 3D design environment (Marx 2000). Reflecting on today's *generation gap* in architecture, Marx believes that clients and competitive demands for efficiency and presentation graphics have created a skill base in architectural practice more dependent on young designers than at any time in history. Older designers' reluctance to learn new computer skills is a prime factor. At the University of California at Berkeley architecture students are using the computer to explore its capabilities for design and presentation. Students are taught a course on digital design, and learn to design *on screen*, without any initial hand sketching. Marx comments that in his experience clients *have a strong desire for realistic images of their project during the earliest stages of design, rather than waiting until the design is almost finished.* Digital design enables this, and advances clients' understanding and involvement. For presentation purposes, Marx believes that digitally based graphic design provides a complex and rich format with which to express those design concepts that can be expressed with words and images, as well as the building design itself. *Digital based graphic design allows the architect to begin to collage ideas, show relationships and build visual concepts.*

12.1   California Center for Contemporary Art
Jerry Jai for University of California, Berkeley, USA 1997

Kristine Fallon (b 1949), elected to the College of Fellows of the American Institute of Architects in recognition of her achievement in applying information technology to architecture, believes design in architecture has been liberated by computer technology. She recognizes however that the predominantly 2D CAD skills of practice will need reshaping for 3D parametric building modelling (Fallon 2000). The emergence of a new generation of architects with three dimensional computer skills will help meet the needs of a changing profession.

12.2   Library for the Information Age
Matthew Schappert for School of Architecture, New Jersey Institute of Technology 1999

The use of electronic tools throughout the design process offers unparalleled convenience, efficiency and trust in communicating information to clients. Ease of modification of drawings has never been simpler. Architects are being encouraged to use software tools to create cross-departmental teams, to share expertise and build on each other's ideas (Gates 2000).

The practice of Nabil Gholam in Beirut was requested to submit a quick design proposal to refurbish the Bell Tower on the Avenue of the Americas. Although working from Beirut, it proved relatively easy to ask a correspondent in New York to take a low resolution digital photograph of the building and send it to Beirut via email. The original photograph was imported into Adobe Photoshop, perspective distortion was adjusted, and the image was resampled to a high resolution. A simple three

dimensional model of the proposed atrium was created and rendered in AutoCAD Release 14 and Accurender 3, including realistic fractal plants. Using Photoshop again, the atrium was composted over the existing photograph and special lighting effects, such as lens flare, were applied on the rendered parts, to fit the actual photograph. The end result, printed and mounted, was presented to the client, *the whole process taking less than one day.* Hence the process of representing and communicating design intention can be very rapid using current technology.

The Internet, a regularly updated medium, encourages collaboration and offers members of a design team the ability to work on same model simultaneously. The concept of *AEC Project Webs* was being heralded as the way ahead, enabling the sharing of drawings and other documents with members of the project team

(Langdon and Williams 2000). Increased bandwidth and hardware speed improvements would contribute to improved Internet capabilities and a shift from two dimensional paper documents to three dimensional web-based project sites.

Some top executives of the CAD industry, attempting to predict likely developments in the 21st century, forecast an increase in acceptance of three dimensional modelling and the possibility of working in a 3D environment from the beginning of the design process (Smith 1999). The use of 3D electronic sketchpads and development of interactive, easy-to-use 3D software were considered essential in assisting creativity. However it was recognized that adoption of three dimensional modelling throughout the design process would require the rethinking of existing work practices and team organization.

12.3   Bell Tower Refurbishment, New York
Ayssar Arida for Nabil Gholam 2000

At the beginning of the 21st century the Internet was increasingly being accepted as an important medium for displaying designs to large audiences. The number of architectural practices using the Internet was increasing (Martin 1999, AJ June 1999). The technology could be secured to restrict the audience to selected viewers, via company intranets. Its capabilities in offering an interactive output medium were being explored by architects who were considering its use alongside video and multi-media compact disk technology.

The range of media for design presentation has never been greater, but this has generated concern about prediction of colour by the multitude of display devices available. Long ago, sources of colour were derived from natural phenomena, some of which were closely guarded secrets. Computers now imitate nature and have palettes of millions of colours. Experience is showing that digital devices are not faithfully reproducing colour images and that a calibration procedure is necessary for high quality colour reproduction (Emmel, Hersc 2000). International researchers and developers are examining key technologies in relation to both the transmission and reproduction of realistic colour images and accurate colour prediction (Macdonald, Luo 1999).

Preoccupation with mastering new skills and technologies, together with ongoing concern for preciseness and efficiency in the design process, may diminish the role of *artistic licence* in architectural representation. Yet Brewster (2000) believes that there will always be a demand for physical display models and high quality perspective drawings as they provide a different aesthetic to the photo-realistic computer model, rather than competing directly. He, with many others, believes that digital visualization needs further recognition as a craft before it can be fully accepted as an architectural presentation method.

Although some architectural offices are exclusively computer-based, many are not. Iain Godwin from **Foster and Partners** says that the practice does not just rely on the digital world for modelling – its in-house model shop is still going on – even though three dimensional computer modelling has grown dramatically (*Building Design* 6 October 2000). Uddin in his study of the use of digital media by 52 architectural practices records that many practices have a hybrid approach, and use a mix of traditional and digital techniques for visualization (Uddin 1999).

The technical pen with India ink and high quality felt tip pens have become part of the signature of our work. These tools, methods, and techniques can be integrated into, and complement the computer graphics of contemporary professional practice. The drawing methods may even offer a therapeutic relief from high-tech practices (Kasprisin, Pettinari 1995).

NORTH ELEVATION   COLUMBIA PUBLIC LIBRARY
                              DANIEL BOONE REGIONAL LIBRARY
                                   COLUMBIA, MISSOURI   HHPA

SOUTH ELEVATION   COLUMBIA PUBLIC LIBRARY
                              DANIEL BOONE REGIONAL LIBRARY
                                   COLUMBIA, MISSOURI   HHPA

Many architects have adopted this *hybrid approach*, combining traditional techniques of drawing, painting and watercolours with digital forms. In America a leading practice **Hardy** (b 1932) **Holzman** (b 1940) **Pfeiffer** (b 1940) **Associates** had a long tradition of presenting their designs to clients as watercolours. James Brogan, formerly Director of Information Technology at HHPA, had been involved with CAD and its integration with architecture for many years. He held a concern that computer images could look generic, and that the character of the firm was missing from many computer-generated presentations. Their practice had developed a style of presentation unique to them, and was keen to ensure computer technology did not detract from this. They developed several different methods of renderings that merged watercolour painting with CAD models, using image-editing software. Images of the Columbia Public Library in Columbia, Missouri, were created by importing a CAD drawing into Photoshop. Colour was added and a scanned watercolour of the sky and trees were edited onto it.

12.4   North Elevation, Columbia Public Library, Missouri
Michael Connolly for Hardy Holzman Pfeiffer Associates 1999

12.5   South Elevation, Columbia Public Library, Missouri
Michael Connolly for Hardy Holzman Pfeiffer Associates 1999

A project by Nabil Gholam had to respond to a client's request for an *artistic impression* of the Lobby of his office building, with variations, all within a very limited budget and short time. A three dimensional computer model was already created, so computer renderings, using Accurender 3, AutoCAD Release 14 and Lightwave, were produced to show different materials options and details. Photoshop was used to merge the computer rendering with people and other details, and also added a vignette effect and a yellowish paper background. The result was printed on an A4 sheet of watercolour paper. A professional artist retouched the printout using watercolours and coloured pencil. Finally the finished image was scanned, enlarged on PC and printed on high resolution photographic paper in A2 size, producing the required result. Ayssar Arida, an architect working for Gholam at the time, commented on the practice's experience *Clients used to be satisfied with 3D. They now want a return to traditional techniques.*

Therefore some architects are finding that clients' expectations have changed since the advent of CAD. Clients may no longer be totally satisfied with basic computer renderings that can appear cold, angular, and without atmosphere. Presentations with an artistic, non-photorealistic quality can be generated with specialist software and still preserve the accuracy expected of computer-generated imagery.

12.6   Corporate Lobby, UAE
Ayssar Arida for Nabil Gholam 2000

The correlation between architectural representation and eventual building has come under renewed interest. *Today, modern architects are rediscovering the joy of sculpting unusual geometries* (Novitski August 2000). The computer's processing capability in structural analysis and production and fabrication techniques is a major contributor to the changing shape of architecture. Architects are exploring *the new possibilities opened up by CAD software, modern analysis and simulation methods, and CAD/CAM construction technology* (Mitchell 2000).

The description and documentation of three dimensional shapes with traditional two dimensional drawings was an obstacle to **Frank Gehry**. He found that two dimensional drawings could sometimes make an unusual design appear more complex than it actually was, and contractors found difficulties in estimating from such documents. *This would result in consideration of alternative designs that could be more successfully communicated through 2D drawing techniques*. In order to surmount this problem, the practice investigated how computer modelling technology and digital measurement could

be applied to their already established *physical model-based* design process.

His experience reflects that traditionally accepted methods of practice could compromise architectural expression. The computer, rather than being a prescriptive tool influencing design intent, could enable the ideas of the architect to be realized. The buildings of Frank Gehry are convincing testimonies that the tools available for design and construction, used appropriately, at different stages of the design process, combined with the creativity and skill of the architect, significantly affect built form.

12.7   Final Design Model, Experience Music Project, Seattle
Frank O Gehry & Associates 1998

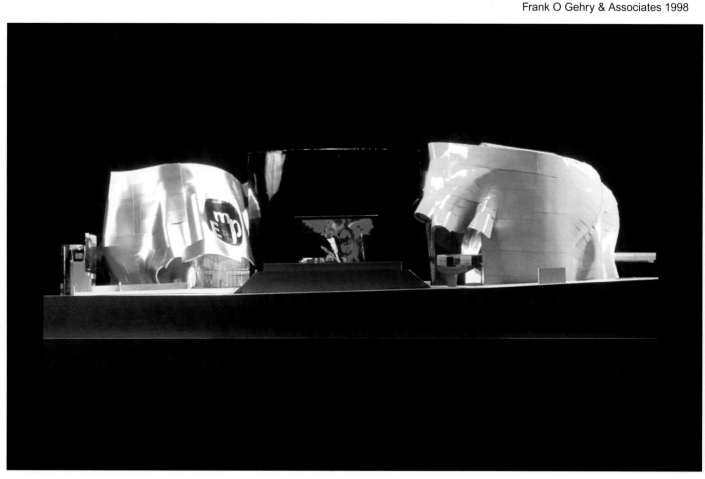

Nicholas Grimshaw was inspired by natural shapes for the design of the Eden Centre, Cornwall, an ecological centre that will be a showcase for global bio-diversity and human dependence on plants. Its shape and structure is based on the geometry of spheres, and intersecting spheres of differing diameters give the impression of a biomorphic organism. This design has enabled the creation of a very lightweight structure of minimal surface and maximum volume. David Kirkland, in a press release from Nicholas Grimshaw & Partners, states, *Today with the power of computers that enable us to manipulate 3D space we are provided with exceptionally powerful tools. How we use these tools will determine the quality of architecture we leave for future generations.*

Creations such as these are exhibits in themselves and certainly demonstrate the possibilities opened up by new design tools and building technologies. Perhaps, more importantly, they demonstrate that it is possible to describe the *essence* of a building through its form.

12.8   Section of Eden Project, Cornwall
Nicholas Grimshaw & Partners 1996

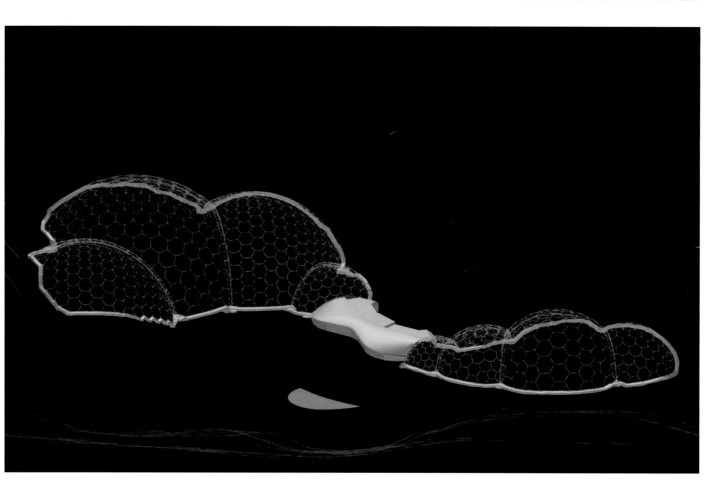

Complex, non-symmetrical geometry, now possible because of computer simulation in the design process, has resulted in debate about the two forms of architecture. In an assessment of contemporary architecture and the nature of form Riley (2000) proposes that *simple, rectilinear geometries and curving topologies (with the exception of certain 'nonorientable' geometries) are now more accurately seen as points on a sliding scale of complexity, rather than as fundamentally different types of forms. If simpler and more complex geometries can be understood as more similar than dissimilar, then we can also see that attempts to judge one or the other on a formal basis alone are not supportable.*

If we apply this line of thought to architectural representation we may consider the digital age as an extension to architectural traditions rather than a contradiction. It may be that the digital tools of today's world will offer distinct advantages in the early stages of design, but traditional methods of representation, with their tactile qualities, will be used alongside digital collages to convey an alternative impression later in the design process. Perhaps traditional media will be considered more appropriate for topographical representations. Whatever the future, new tools and techniques that extend choice and enhance architectural freedom will be welcomed. *It is not that, in the age of information processing, tradition or tradition rooted forms of human practice cease; they are complemented by new forms, some impractical or even impossible in previous paradigms of thinking and creating* (Nadin 1989). The past holds many examples of traditions revived to meet the needs of architectural influences of particular periods. Model making has had a very long history, but was chosen as the appropriate form of representation during the Modern Movement. *White*

cardboard models, miniaturized, presented and proliferated the new International Style – causing the model-maker's craft to be mirrored in a built architecture stripped of ornamentation (Porter 1997).

The role of two dimensional and three dimensional modes of representation has fluctuated throughout history. New techniques have emerged, but never entirely replaced their precedents. With so much discussion today about the powerful editing facilities of computer software, it is easy to overlook the long established convenience of the humble pencil and eraser, and their role in supporting an easy-to-use, interactive environment between architect and sketchbook. It is unlikely that this will ever disappear.

The computer is undoubtedly more than a presentation tool, and its capabilities as a design tool are increasingly recognized. Yet it is a relative newcomer in the long line of tools, media and techniques that have influenced the built environment. Fellows, in considering the role of drawing in architecture and the architect's work, concludes by saying *If there is a message, it is that the relationship between drawing and architectural design is very close. The architect thinks through drawings and they reflect design theory and process. Drawings are not a mere representation or a means to an end. This must be remembered in our CAD-age* (Fellows 1998).

As the profession masters any new tools and techniques we see their influence in built form. Gothic architecture would not have been possible without the rediscovery of Euclidean geometry. The 15th century saw a wide use of paper for the first time, offering a cheaper alternative to the vellum and parchment of past eras. The printing press was developed, and was significant in

introducing the ideas of masters to others. Some early illustrations in *Artists' Impressions* reflect the architect's intention to publish, and the layout of presentations reflects this purpose. The period of the Renaissance introduced techniques, media and tools that liberated the draughtsman and enabled greater freedom of expression. Minute details of a building façade could be drawn with fine pencils, graphite, pen and ink. Gentler tones and effects could be added with crayon, charcoal and chalk. New media contributed greatly to artistic output and built form of precise geometry and fine detail.

Smythson's precise drawings of the 16th century demonstrate careful use of dividers and compasses. **Talman** used one point perspective techniques in the 17th century, and demonstrated early penmanship with clear lines and blacking in. **Campbell** demonstrated the technique of sciagraphy in the 18th century, and his pen and wash techniques showed clearly the curves for both the dome and vaults of his design for Mereworth Castle. **Gandy** skilfully utilized pencil, watercolour and rendered perspective techniques to demonstrate the lighting effects of **Soane**'s designs. Some of Gandy's designs in the early 19th century demonstrated his fascination with circular forms produced by his compass (Hambly 1982). The designs of **Shaw** would have been very difficult without use of a tee-square and protractor, and his black and white techniques were particularly appropriate for the new printing techniques of the time. The popular bird's-eye view of the 20th century had been by used Harding in his view of Crystal Palace for Joseph **Paxton**. Specialist pens aided the worm's-eye view of **Stirling**'s axonometrics. The watercolours of Cyril **Farey** for Edwin **Lutyens** were so full of realism that you could almost walk through the building.

So we question whether the school of thought, that the relationship between drawing and architectural design is very close, may be extended to other forms of representation, such as painting, sculpture, physical or computer model making. The answer must be yes, but dependent on the architect being skilful and relaxed with his chosen medium of design, which *may be different to the medium of presentation.* This distinction is important. When architects work in harmony with the tools and media available, with focus on the design itself rather than medium of its representation, then interaction is possible and creative ideas can be displayed. The method of representation should be close to the designer's own mental representation, and enable an intimate process to develop between medium and mental idea. *Artists' Impressions* have identified several such instances. **Le Corbusier** believed profoundly that his painting was crucial for his understanding of architecture. Coloured pens were **Frank Lloyd Wright**'s favourite medium. The fluent and delicate penmanship of Pugin provided the required Gothic detailing for designs of his time. Frank Gehry's ideas are communicated initially via physical models prior to his digital design process. Yet modelling with any physical media requires a separation between the user and the modelling medium, which calls for deliberate, self-conscious planning (Russ 1997). It is the *what–if* exploratory nature of computer modelling that introduces flexibility and openness, and allows for revision of those initial properties selected to preserve in the representation.

A historical perspective is valuable in any analysis of representation today. If we consider the computer solely as a medium for representation, then it impressively adds to a rich collection of presentation aids that have developed over the years. If we consider the computer as a design tool then it is its speed and mathematical ability that single it out from design tools of the past. Medieval cathedrals took centuries to build, and their originators never saw the completed form. Today successful architects can see many of their projects realized in built form, some of which are heralding a new architecture on the sliding scale of complexity described by Riley.

Evolution or revolution? The difference is one of timescale. In an attempt to analyse the underlying factors for differing styles and techniques, in addition to the personal taste of the architect, we can identify several contributors. Scientific innovation, availability of tools, new materials, economics, transportation, education and clients' expectations each play a part. In relation to the tools of representation developed over the ages, five hundred years elapsed between the invention of the compass and the introduction of the photocopier. The previous two chapters of *Artists' Impressions* have outlined tremendous changes in technological progress over the last thirty years. So whilst architects have always been faced with the advancement of technology, today's changes may be considered revolutionary and reflect the magnitude of change which occurred with the introduction of perspective.

Some architects have embraced this technological progress, adapting it to fit within traditional work practices, in the hope that it will aid and improve. Others have been reluctant to accept it at all, preferring to run their practices using established traditions. Those who have given innovation a chance are discovering that its potential is much greater than simply providing new tools to solve old problems. To gain the maximum potential from the technology available today requires change. Spiller believes that as technology continues to advance, architectural practice is further fragmented. *The more adventurous and interesting architects are starting to redefine their professional parameters: theirs is a trajectory of training and retraining.* (Architectural Design Nov/Dec 1998). Yet *we must consider that architecture is in its very essence a conservative art and perhaps cannot leave its accustomed tracks as easily as painting or the applied arts. For a building is always of considerably greater economic importance; its practical realization requires thorough preparation and depends on a multitude of external conditions with which the other arts need not concern themselves. Of all the arts, the building is the most ponderous* (Muthesius 1994).

Computerization is revolutionizing society, the construction industry, architectural practice and the envisioning of buildings. Perhaps the greatest challenge to architects today is how to adopt the best of both worlds, to use appropriately both traditional and new creative media. The careful selection of visualization methods from the wide range now available could result in architecture of great quality and diversity. Ultimately it could be a heterogeneity of techniques that will produce the best representation of our future architecture.

List of Illustrations

6   Three Dimensional Drawings

7   Thin Straight Lines

8   Realistic Impressions

9   Models

10   Computer-Aided Design

11   Virtual Reality

12   Where Next? Ideas and Conclusions

Credits

Arup Associates: Fig. 11.7 © Hayes Davidson

Avery Architectural and Fine Arts Library, Columbia University in the City of New York: Fig. 6.5

Bartlett School of Architecture, University College London: Fig. 12.0 Christian Groothuizen. Instructor Neil Spiller

Bibliothèque Nationale, Institut de France: Fig. 3.1 MS 2184; BN 2037, f. 5v.

British Architectural Library, Drawings Collection, Royal Institute of British Architects: Figs 2.1, 3.0, 3.2, 3.3, 3.4, 3.5, 3.6, 3.7, 3.8, 3.9, 3.15, 3.16, 3.17, 3.18, 3.20, 4.0, 4.1, 4.4, 4.5, 4.6, 4.7, 4.8, 4.9, 4.10, 4.11, 4.12, 4.13, 4.14, 4.15, 4.16, 4.17, 4.18, 4.19, 4.20, 5.0, 5.1, 5.2, 5.4, 5.10, 5.11, 5.12, 5.13, 6.1, 6.8, 6.11, 6.17, 6.18, 6.19, 7.0, 7.1, 7.2, 7.3, 7.4, 7.5, 7.6, 7.7, 7.8, 7.9, 7.10, 7.11, 7.12, 7.13, 7.14, 7.21, 7.22, 8.0, 8.1, 8.2, 8.3, 8.4, 8.5, 8.7, 8.8, 8.9, 8.10, 8.11, 8.12, 8.13, 8.14, 8.15, 8.18, 9.0, 9.3, 9.7, 9.8, 9.16, 9.17, 9.18, 9.19, 10.0, 10.4 Fig. 10.0 Courtesy of Arup Associates, Computer Illustrators Stephen Miller, Jeanelle Plummer, John Hare; Fig. 10.4 Courtesy of Skidmore Owings and Merrill. Computer Illustrator Carrie Byles

Building Design Partnership: Fig. 10.11

Burrell Collection, Glasgow: Figs 5.9, 9.22 © Glasgow Museums

Centre for Advanced Studies in Architecture, University of Bath: Figs 10.6, 11.1 Fig. 11.1 Courtesy of Chapman Taylor

Cesar Pelli & Associates Inc.: Figs 10.12, 10.13 Fig. 10.13 CG Drawing: Sight Corp.

Codrington Library, All Souls College, Oxford: Figs 3.10, 3.11, 3.12 The Warden and Fellows of All Souls College, Oxford

Derek Lovejoy Partnership: Fig. 10.16 Martin Kelly, Mark Martin. Collaborating architect GMW.

DES Architects and Engineers: Fig. 10.10 Project Principal Susan Eschweiler, Senior Project Designer John Marx

Eindhoven University of Technology: Fig. 11.3

Erith and Terry: Figs 5.5, 6.0, 9.26

FaulknerBrowns: Figs 6.15, 6.16, 10.15 Fig. 10.15 Andrew Hilton

Fondation Le Corbusier: Figs 7.15, 7.16, 7.17, 9.12, 9.13, 9.14, 9.15

Form 4 Architects: Fig. 10.17 Principal in Charge – Robert Giannini, Design Principals – John Marx/Paul Ferro, Graphic Design – Wilson Auyeung

Foster and Partners: Figs 10.22, 11.8 Photography by Richard Davies

Frank O Gehry & Associates: Figs 10.8, 12.7

Frank Lloyd Wright Foundation: Figs 5.3, 6.2, 6.4, 9.11 The drawings of Frank Lloyd Wright are Copyright © 2000, The Frank Lloyd Wright Foundation, Scottsdale, AZ.

Glasgow School of Art Collection: Fig. 4.21

Hardy Holzman Pfeiffer Associates: Figs 12.4, 12.5 Michael Connolly

Hayes Davidson: Figs 10.23, 10.24, 11.7 Fig. 10.23 Courtesy of James Stirling Michael Wilford and Associates; Fig. 10.24 Courtesy of Richard Rogers Partnership; Fig. 11.7 Courtesy of Arup Associates

Ian Ritchie Architects: Figs 10.18, 10.19

Insite Environments: Figs 11.2, 11.4 Fig. 11.2 Courtesy of Miller Homes; Fig. 11.4 Courtesy of North Tyneside Challenge

James Stirling, Michael Wilford and Associates: Figs 5.16, 6.9, 6.10, 10.23 Fig. 6.10 © James Stirling Foundation Archive; Fig. 10.23 © Hayes Davidson

Jeremy Dixon, Edward Jones and Carl Laubin: Figs 8.16, 8.17

Library St Paul's Cathedral: Figs 9.1, 9.2

London Borough of Lambeth Archives Department: Fig. 3.19

MacCormac Jamieson Pritchard: Figs 5.6, 5.7, 5.8, 9.25 Fig. 9.25 Steve Haryott of Enterprise Models and Photographer Peter Durant

Metropolitan Cathedral of Christ the King, Liverpool: Fig. 8.6

Michael Hopkins and Partners: Fig. 10.1

MUSE Virtual Presence: Figs 11.0, 11.12 Fig. 11.0 Courtesy of J Sainsbury plc; Fig. 11.12 Courtesy of University of Manchester

Museum of Modern Art, New York: Figs 6.6, 6.7, 7.18, 7.19, 7.20, 9.10, 9.11, 9.20, 9.21

Fig. 6.6: MEIER, Richard. The Atheneum. New Harmony, Indiana. 1979. Perspective. Pencil on paper, 15 × 15″ (38 × 38cm). The Museum of Modern Art, New York. Gift of the architect. Photograph © 2000 The Museum of Modern Art, New York.

Fig. 6.7: MEIER, Richard. Museum of Contemporary Art. Barcelona, Spain. 1987. Exterior perspective. Silkscreen, 29⅝ × 29⅞″ (75.3 × 75.9cm). The Museum of Modern Art, New York. Gift of the architect in honor of Philip Johnson. Photograph © 2000 The Museum of Modern Art, New York.

Fig. 7.18: MIES van der ROHE, Ludwig. Farnsworth House. Fox River, Plano, Illinois. 1946. North elevation. Preliminary version. Pencil, watercolor on tracing paper, 13 × 25″ (33 × 63.5cm). The Mies van der Rohe Archive. The Museum of Modern Art, New York. Gift of the architect. Photograph © 2000 The Museum of Modern Art, New York.

Fig. 7.19: MIES van der ROHE, Ludwig. Seagram Building. 375 Park Avenue, New York. 1954–58. Plaza sculpture. Partial elevation. Pencil on paper, photostat cut-out attached. 42¼ × 177″ (107.9 × 534.4cm). The Mies van der Rohe Archive, The Museum of Modern Art, New York. Gift of the architect. Photograph © 2000 The Museum of Modern Art, New York.

Fig. 7.20: MIES van der ROHE, Ludwig. Apartment Buildings, 860/880 Lake Shore Drive, Chicago, Illinois.

1948–51. Exterior perspective. Pencil on note paper, 21 × 33¾″ (53.3 × 88.3cm). The Mies van der Rohe Archive. The Museum of Modern Art, New York. Gift of the architect. Photograph © 2000 The Museum of Modern Art, New York.

Fig. 9.9: WRIGHT, Frank Lloyd. Frederick C. Robie House, Chicago, Illinois. 1906–1909. Model by G. Loyd Barnum, 15 × 48 × 37½″ (38.1 × 122 × 95.2cm). The Museum of Modern Art, New York. Exhibition Fund, 1938. Photograph © 2000 The Museum of Modern Art.

Fig. 9.10: WRIGHT, Frank Lloyd. 'Falling Water', Edgar Kaufmann House, Bear Run, Pennsylvania. 1935–37. Model by Paul Bonfilio with Joseph Zelvin, Larry List and Edith Randel, 1984. Mixed media, 40½ × 71½ × 47¹∨₂″ (103 × 181.5 × 121cm). The Museum of Modern Art, New York. Best Products Company Architecture Fund. Photograph © 2000 The Museum of Modern Art, New York.

Fig. 9.20: GEHRY, Frank. Winton Guest House. Wayzata, Michigan. 1983–1986. Model. Wood, plastic, plaster, 11¾ × 24 × 24″ (29.8 × 61 × 61cm). The Museum of Modern Art, New York. Gift of the architect. Photograph © 2000 The Museum of Modern Art, New York.

Fig. 9.21: MEIER, Richard. Federal Building and U.S. Courthouse. Islip, New York. 1993. Model. Wood, 34 × 50¼ × 26¼″ (86.3 × 127.7 × 66.7cm). The Museum of Modern Art, New York. Gift of the architect in honor of Philip Johnson. Photograph © 2000 The Museum of Modern Art, New York.

Nabil Gholam: Figs 10.14, 11.5, 12.3, 12.6 Figs 10.14, 12.3 Ayssar Arida; Fig. 12.6 Ayssar Arida. Nextvision Beirut. Joseph Abou Khalil; Fig. 11.5 AXYZ 3D consultants. Aerial view courtesy of MAPS Lebanon

Nicholas Grimshaw & Partners: Figs 5.20, 5.21, 9.28, 10.9, 12.8

Ricardo Bofill: Fig. 10.5 Nabil Gholam, Scott Dimit. Courtesy of Taller Paris

Richard Rogers Partnership: Figs 5.14, 5.15, 6.12, 9.23, 9.24, 10.20, 10.21, 10.24, 11.6 Fig. 9.23 Andrew Holmes; Fig. 9.24 John Donat Photography; Fig. 10.24. © Hayes Davidson

Rob Becker: Fig. 8.21

School of Architecture, New Jersey Institute of Technology: Figs 11.11, 11.13, 12.2 Fig. 11.11 Mariko Fujitsuka. Instructor/Design Critic Professor Glenn Goldman; Fig. 11.13 Samantha Hockins. Instructor/Design Critic Professor Glenn Goldman; Fig. 12.2 Matthew Schappert. Instructor/Design Critic Professor Glenn Goldman

Sir John Soane's Museum: Figs 4.2, 4.3, 9.4, 9.5, 9.6

Terry Farrell and Partners: Figs 5.17, 5.18, 5.19, 6.13, 6.14, 8.19, 9.27

Tom Schaller: Fig. 8.20

Uncredited: Figs 2.0, 3.13, 3.14

University of California, Berkeley USA: Fig. 12.1 Jerry Jai. Instructor John Marx

YRM: Figs 10.2, 10.3, 10.7, 11.9, 11.10 Fig. 10.2 Computer Illustrators Hugh Whitehead, Linda Scott; Fig. 10.3 Computer Illustrator Hugh Whitehead; Figs 10.7, 11.9 Computer Illustrator Graham Cook

References

Books

Ackerman, J.S. *Palladio* Harmondsworth: Penguin Books, 1966

Ahrends, P., Burton, R., Koralek, P. *Ahrends Burton and Koralek* London: Academy Editions, 1991

Alberti, L.B. *De Re Aedificatoria: Ten Books on Architecture*, 1485, translated into Italian by Bartoli, C. and into English by Leoni, J. London: Alec Tiranti, 1955

Arnell, P., Bickford, T. (eds) *Frank Gehry: Buildings and Projects* New York: Rizzoli, 1985

Aslet, C. *Quinlan Terry: The Revival of Architecture* Harmondsworth: Penguin Books, 1986

Banham, M., Hillier, B. (eds) *A Tonic to the Nation: The Festival of Britain 1951* London: Thames and Hudson, 1976

Barbaro, D. *La Practica della Perspectiva* Venetia: B&R Borgominieri, 1569

Bartlett, B. *et al. Architectural Rendering* Berkeley: New Riders, 1996

Betjeman, J. *First and Last Loves* London: Murray, 1952

Binney, M. *Palace on the River* London: Wordsearch Publishing Ltd., 1991

Blake, P. *The Master Builders 1960, Le Corbusier, Mies van der Rohe, Frank Lloyd Wright* Harmondsworth: Pelican Books, 1963

Blaser, W. *Mies van der Rohe: Continuing the Chicago School of Architecture* 1977 Basel, Boston, Stuttgart: Birkhauser, 1981

Blaser, W. *Richard Meier Details* Basel: Birkhauser Verlag, 1996

Blomfield, R.T. *Architectural Drawing and Draughtsmen* London: Cassell and Co., 1912

Booth, P., Taylor, N. *Cambridge New Architecture* London: Leonard Hill, 1970

Boucher, B. *Andrea Palladio: The Architect in his Time* New York: Abbeville Publishers, 1994

Boulton, A.O. *Frank Lloyd Wright: Architect – An Illustrated Biography* New York: Rizzoli, 1993

Brandon-Jones, J. 'CFA Voysey' in Ferriday, P. (ed.) *Victorian Architecture* London: Jonathan Cape, 1963

Bridges, A. *The Construction Net* London: E & FN Spon, 1996

Bruschi, A. *Bramante* London: Thames and Hudson, 1977

Buchanan, P. *Renzo Piano Building Workshop* Complete works vol. 1, London: Phaidon Press Limited, 1993

Burckhardt, J. *The Architecture of the Italian Renaissance* translated by Palmes, J., revised and edited by Murray, P. Harmondsworth: Penguin Books, 1987

Burri, R. *Le Corbusier: Magnum Photos* Basel: Birkhauser, 1999

Cantacuzino, S. *Wells Coates: A Monograph* London: Gordon Fraser, 1978

Carter, P. *Mies van der Rohe at Work* London: The Pall Mall Press, 1974

Chambers, W. *A Treatise on the Decorative Part of Civil Architecture* London: 1791, republished by Gregg International Publishers Ltd., 1969

Clark, A.G. 'AWN Pugin' in Ferriday, P. (ed.) *Victorian Architecture* London: Jonathan Cape, 1963

Coe, P., Reading, M. *Lubetkin and Tecton: Architecture and Social Commitment* London: The Arts Council of Great Britain, 1981

Cole, D. 'Sir Gilbert Scott' in Ferriday, P. (ed.) *Victorian Architecture* London: Jonathan Cape, 1963

Connors, J. *The Robie House of Frank Lloyd Wright* Chicago: University Press, 1984

Cook, P. *Artrandom: Conversations* Kyoto: Shoin International Co. Ltd., 1990

Cook, P., Llewellyn-Jones, R. *New Spirit in Architecture* New York: Rizzoli, 1991

Cunningham, C., Waterhouse, P. *Alfred Waterhouse 1830–1905* Oxford: Clarendon Press, 1992

Diekman, N., Pile, J. *Drawing Interior Architecture* New York: Watson-Guptill Publications, 1983

Dodd, E.M. 'Charles Robert Cockerell' in Ferriday, P (ed.) *Victorian Architecture* London: Jonathan Cape, 1963

Downes, K. *The Architecture of Wren* Granada Publishing, 1982, 2nd ed., Redhedge, 1988

Drexler, A. *Ludwig Mies van der Rohe* New York: George Braziller Inc., 1960

Drexler, A. *The Drawings of Frank Lloyd Wright* New York: Horizon Press, 1962

Dudley, G.A. *A Workshop for Peace: Designing the United Nations Headquarters* The Architectural History Foundation, Inc., Cambridge, Mass.: MIT Press, 1994

Dunster, D. (ed.) *Alison + Peter Smithson: The Shift* Architectural Monographs 7, London: Academy Editions, 1982

Emanuel, M. *Contemporary Architects* London: St. James Press, 3rd ed. 1994

Esher, L. *A Broken Wave: The Rebuilding of England 1940–1980* London: Allen Lane, Penguin Books Ltd., 1981

Farey, C.A., Edwards, A.T. *Architectural Drawing, Perspective and Rendering* 1931, 2nd ed. 1949

Farrish, W. *Isometrical Perspective*, 1820

Fellows, R. *Edwardian Architecture: Style and Technology* London: Lund Humphries, 1995

Fleetwood-Hesketh, P., 'Sir Charles Barry' in Ferriday, P. (ed.) *Victorian Architecture* London Jonathan Cape, 1963

Foley, J.D. *et al. Computer Graphics Principles and Practice* London: Addison Wesley Longman 1993

Foster, N. *et al. Foster Associates: Buildings and Projects* vol. 2 1971–1978, Hong Kong Watermark Publications, 1989

Fowler, J., Cornforth J. *English Decoration in the 18th Century* London: Barrie and Jenkins, 1974 2nd ed. 1978

Fry, M. *Autobiographical Sketches* London: Elek Books Ltd, 1975

Gates, W. *The Road Ahead* Harmondsworth: Penguin Books, 1996

Gates, W. *Business @ the Speed of Thought: Succeeding in the Digital Economy* New York Warner Books, 2000

Gibbs, J. *A Book of Architecture* London, 1728, republished, New York: Benjamin Blom, 1968

Girouard, M. *Robert Smythson and the Architecture of the Elizabethan Era* London: Country Life 1966

Glancey, J. *New British Architecture* London: Thames and Hudson, 1989

Goodhart-Rendel, H.S. 'The Country House of the 19th Century' in Ferriday, P. (ed.) *Victorian Architecture* London: Jonathan Cape, 1963

Gradidge, R. 'Edwin Lutyens: The Last High Victorian' in Fawcett, J. (ed.) *Seven Victorian Architects* London: Thames and Hudson, 1976

Green, L.J. (ed.) *Richard Meier Architect* vol. 3 1992–1999, New York: Rizzoli International Publications Inc., 1999

Guinness, D., Sadler, J.T. *The Palladian Style* London: Thames and Hudson, 1976

Hambly, M. *Drawing Instruments: Their History, Purpose and Use for Architectural Drawings* Harris, J.(Foreword), London: RIBA, 1982

Harris, J. *Sir William Chambers* New Haven: Yale University Press, 1996 (first published London 1970)

Harris, J. *The Palladians* London: Trefoil Books, 1981

Harris, J. *William Talman: Maverick Architect* London and Boston: George, Allen and Unwin 1982

Hart, V. *St. Paul's Cathedral: Sir Christopher Wren* London Phaidon Press Ltd., 1995

Haslam, R. *Clough Williams-Ellis* London: Academy Editions, 1996

Hellman, L. *Archi-tetes: the Id in the Grid* Chichester: Wiley-Academy, 2000

Hitchcock, H.-R. *The Pelican History of Art: Architecture, Nineteenth and Twentieth Centuries* Harmondsworth: Penguin Books, 1958 4th ed. 1977

Hitchmough, W. *CFA Voysey* London: Phaidon Press Ltd., 1995

Hohauser, S. *Architectural and Interior Models: design and construction* New York: Van Nostrand, 1970

Howell, W.G., Killick, J., Partridge, J., Amis, SW. *Architecture* London: Lund Humphries, 1981

Jenkins, E. 'The Victorian Architectural Profession' in Ferriday, P. (ed.) *Victorian Architecture* London: Jonathan Cape, 1963

Jodidio, P. *Contemporary American Architects* vol. IV, New York: Taschen, 1998

Jopling, J. *The Practice of Isometrical Perspective* London: M. Taylor, 1835

Kasprisin, R., Pettinari, J. *Visual Thinking for Architects and Designers* New York: Van Nostrand Reinhold, 1995

Kaye, B.L.B. *The Development of the Architectural Profession in England: A Sociological Study* London: George Allen and Unwin, 1960

Kinnard, J., 'GE Street, The Law Courts and the Seventies' in Ferriday, P. (ed.) *Victorian Architecture* London: Jonathan Cape, 1963

Latham, I., Swenarton, M., Sampson, P. *Sketchbook 12.05.98 Terry Farrell and Partners* London: Right Angle Publishing Ltd., 1998

Le Corbusier *Towards A New Architecture* 1923, translated by Etchells, F. 1927, London: Architectural Press, 1946

Lees-Milne, J. *The Age of Inigo Jones* London: Batsford, 1953

Lever, J., Richardson, M. *Great Drawings from the Collection of the Royal Institute of British Architects* London: Trefoil Books, 1983

Little, B. *Sir Christopher Wren: A Historical Biography* London: Robert Hale, 1975

Lyon, D. *Le Corbusier Alive* Paris: Vilo International, 2000

McCarthy, T. *Reekie's Architectural Drawing* 4th ed. New York: John Wiley & Sons, 1996 (first published 1946)

Macdonald, L.W., Luo, R. *Colour Imaging Vision and Technology* London: John Wiley & Sons, 1999

Manser, J. *Hugh Casson: A Biography* Harmondsworth: Penguin Books, 2000

Martin, J.L. *Buildings and Ideas* Cambridge: The University Press, 1983

Meier, R. *Buildings and Projects 1966–1976* New York: Oxford University Press, 1976

Meier, R. *Barcelona Museum of Contemporary Art* New York: The Monacelli Press, 1997

Middleton, R. (ed.) *The Beaux-Arts* London: Thames and Hudson, 1982

Morgan, A.L., Naylor, C. (eds) *Contemporary Architects* London: St. James Press, 1987

Morgan, M.H. *Vitruvius: The Ten Books on Architecture* Cambridge Mass.: Harvard University Press, 1914

Muthesius, H. *Style-architecture and Building-art: Transformations of Architecture in the Nineteenth Century and its Present Condition* Chicago: University Press, 1994

Myerscough-Walker, R. *The Perspectivist* London: Sir Isaac Pitman and Sons, Ltd., 1958

Pace, P. *The Architecture of George Pace* London: BT Batsford Ltd., 1990

Palmes, J.C. *Sir Banister Fletcher's A History of Architecture* 18th ed. London: The Athlone Press, 1975

Perez-Gomez, A., Pelletier, L. *Architectural Representation and the Perspective Hinge* London: The MIT Press, 1997

Perouse de Montclos, J-M. *Etienne-Louis Boullée, 1728–1799, Theoretician of Revolutionary Architecture* London: Thames and Hudson, 1974

Pevsner, N. 'Richard Norman Shaw' in Ferriday, P. (ed.) *Victorian Architecture* London: Jonathan Cape, 1963

Porter, T. *The Architect's Eye* London: E&FN Spon, 1997

Powell, K. *Richard Rogers Complete Works* vol. 1, London: Phaidon Press, 1999

Puppi, L. *Andrea Palladio* London: Phaidon, 1975

Rheingold, H. *Virtual Reality* London: Secker & Warburg, 1991

Richardson, M. *Sketches by Edwin Lutyens: RIBA Drawings* Monographs no. 1, London: Academy Editions, 1994

Riley, T., Reid, P. (eds) *Frank Lloyd Wright, Architect* New York: Museum of Modern Art, 1994

Riley, T. *10x10 Thinking Towards a New Architecture* London: Phaidon Press Limited, 2000

Ruegg, A. *Le Corbusier* Basel: Birkhauser Publishers, 1999

Saint, A. *The Image of the Architect* New Haven and London: Yale University Press, 1983

Schaller, T.W. *The Art of Architectural Drawing: Imagination & Technique* New York: Van Nostrand Reinhold, 1997

Serlio, S. *The Book of Architecture* London: Robert Peake, 1611, translated out of Italian into Dutch and out of Dutch into English, New York: Benjamin Blom Inc., 1970

Shaw, R.N. *Architectural Sketches from the Continent* London: Publicity for the Proprietors, 1858

Shaw, R.N., Jackson, T.G. (eds) *Architecture: A Profession or an Art? Thirteen Short Essays on the Qualification and Training of Architects*, London: J. Murray, 1892

Spiers, R.P. *Architectural Drawing* London: Cassell and Co., 1887

Spiller, N. *10x10 The Eclectic Fractured Future for Architecture* London: Phaidon Press Limited, 2000

Stamp, G. *The Great Perspectivists* London: Royal Institute of British Architects, 1982

Stephan, R. (ed.) *Eric Mendelsohn, Architect 1887–1953* New York: The Monacelli Press, 1999

Stirling, J. *Buildings and Projects 1950–1974* London: Thames and Hudson, 1975

Summerson, J. *Architecture in Britain 1530–1830* 8th ed. Harmondsworth: Penguin, 1991 (first published 1953)

Summerson, J. *Heavenly Mansions* London: The Cresset Press, 1949

Summerson, J. *Inigo Jones* Harmondsworth: Penguin, 1966

Sutherland, I.E. *Sketchpad: A Man-Machine Graphical Communications System* Baltimore: Spartan Books, 1963

Tavernor, R. *Palladio and Palladianism* London: Thames and Hudson, 1991

Uddin, M. Saleh *Digital Architecture* London: McGraw-Hill, 1999

Whinney, M. *Wren* London: Thames and Hudson, 1971

Whittick, A. *Eric Mendelsohn* London: Leonard Hill Books Ltd 1940, 2nd ed. 1956

Wilford, M., Muirhead, T., Maxwell, R. *James Stirling, Michael Wilford and Associates Buildings and Projects* London: Thames and Hudson, 1994

Williams-Ellis, C. *Portmeirion: The Place and its Meaning* Portmerion, Penrhyndeudraeth, 1963, revised ed. 1973

Wilson, M.I. *William Kent: Architect, Designer, Painter, Gardener* London: Routledge & Kegan Paul, 1984

Windsor, A. *Peter Behrens: Architect and Designer 1868–1940* London: The Architectural Press Ltd., 1981

Wren Society *The Wren Society: Thirteenth Volume* Oxford: University Press, 1936

Wright, F.L. *An Autobiography* New York: Longman Green and Co., 1932

Zevi, B. *Eric Mendelsohn: The Complete Works* Basel: Birkhauser Publishers, 1999

Periodicals

Adams, M.B. 'Architectural Drawing' *Building News*, XLVIII, 6 February 1901, pp 204–6

AlSayyad, N. 'Virtual Cairo: An Urban Historian's View of Computer Simulation' *Leonardo,* vol. 32, no. 2, pp 93–100, 1996

Battle, G., McCarthy, C. 'Multi-Source Synthesis Interactive Urbanism' *Architectural Design*, November/December 1994, vol. 64, no. 11/12, pp ii–vii

Boesjes, E.M. 'Computer-Video Animation' *CADENCE*, Jan 1993, pp 72–4

Broadbent, G. 'Representing Architecture', *Architectural Design*, vol. 59, no. 3/4 March/April 1989, pp 1–89

Buday, R. 'Architects Blend Traditional Design with New Media' *ArchitectureWeek*, August 2000, p T1.1

Claridge, R. 'Rendering: Then and Now' *CADENCE*, August 1996, pp 28–30

Clary, L. 'Virtual Cranbrook Unites Tradition and Technology' *ArchitectureWeek*, July 2000, p T1.1

Conlon, T. 'Green CAD and 3D Design Survey' *ArchitectureWeek*, July 2000, p T2.2

Coyne, R. 'The Implications of Heidegger's Thinking for Computer Representations' *Leonardo,* vol. 27, no. 1, 1994, pp 65–73

Crosbie, M.J. 'Norman Foster: Analog and Digital Ecology' *ArchitectureWeek*, no. 19, September 2000

Dupont, P. 'Overview of Current Virtual Reality Applications' *Information Processing '94*, vol. III, 1994, vol. 53, ch. 82, pp 159–62

Elias, H., Rogers, L 'Old Hat Architects Set to Turn to Computers; Are you up to IT?' *RIBA Journal*, vol. 104, no. 7, July 1997, pp 4, 6–7, 9

Fallon, K. 'Looking for Higher Technology Benefits' *Architectural Record*, vol. 186, no. 12, December 1998, pp 139–42

Goodhart-Rendel, H.S. 'Architectural Draughtsmanship of the Past' Lecture to RIBA 9 January 1951 and *RIBA Journal* 3rd Series, LVIII, 1951, p 127

Hayward, D. 'A Vision of the Future', *New Civil Engineer*, February 1993

Howes, J. 'IT: Survey of Computer Use 1994' *RIBA Journal*, vol. 102, no. 1, p 62, Jan 1995

Jayaram, S. 'Virtual Reality' *Computer Aided Design,* 1997, vol. 29, no. 8, pp 543–5

Jones, B., 'Computer Imagery: Imitation and Representation of Realities' *Leonardo, Computer Art in Context Supplement Issue*, 1989, pp 31–8

Langdon, G.M., Williams, A. 'A Trend to be Reckoned With – AEC Project Webs' *CADENCE*, February 2000

Lipstadt, H. 'Architecture and its Image' *Architectural Design*, vol. 59, no. 3/4, March/April 1989, pp 1–89

Lyall, S. 'An Aye for Detail' *Design Week,* March 21 1997, pp 68–9

Manisty, M. 'Virtual Reality on the Web' *Construction Computing*, July/August 1997

Martin, I. 'Architects take Pole Position in IT Use' *Building Design*, no. 1399, 11 June 1999, p 5

Marx, J. 'A Proposal for Alternative Methods for Teaching Digital Design' *Automation in Construction*, September 2000, pp 19–35

Miller, G. *et al.* 'The Virtual Museum: Interactive 3D Navigation of a Multimedia Database' *The Journal of Visualisation and Computer Animation,* 1992, vol. 3, pp 183–97

Mitchell, W. 'Square Ideas' *New Scientist*, February 2000, p 52

Monnier, G. 'Perspective, Axonometric et Rapport au Réel' *Techniques et Architecture*, no. 358, 1985, pp 120–3

Nadin, M. 'Emergent Aesthetics – Aesthetic Issues in Computer Art' *Leonardo, Computer Art in Context Supplement Issue*, 1989, pp 43–8

Novitski, B.J. 'Digital Architect Giving Small Firms the Tools to be Big' *Architectural Record*, vol. 188, no. 2, February 2000, pp 141–2

Novitski, B.J. 'Fun with Computer-Aided Modeling Clay' *ArchitectureWeek*, August 2000, p T3.1

Pickering, J. 'Cyberspace and the Architecture of Power' *Architectural Design*, vol. 66, no. 3/4 March/April 1996, pp vi–xi

Ray-Jones, A. 'CICA 89' *RIBA Journal*, vol. 97, no. 1, January 1990, pp 107–8

Richens, P., Trinder, M. 'Design Participation through the Internet: a Case Study; Architects: RMJM' *ARQ: Architectural Research Quarterly*, vol. 3, no. 4, 1999, pp 361–74

Romero, C. 'Vortex 2000' *Architectural Design*, vol. 68, no. 11/12, 1998, pp 46–51

Russ, S. 'Empirical Modelling: the Computer as a Modelling Medium' *Computer Bulletin*, April 1997, pp 20–2

Smith, S. 'Design for the New Millennium' *CADALYST*, November 1999

Spiller, N. 'Unit 19: Restless Hearts and Restless Minds' *Architectural Design*, vol. 68, no. 11/12, 1998, pp 86–91

Stone, R. 'A Year in the Life of British Virtual Reality' *Virtual Reality World*, 2(1), 1994, pp 48–62

Swenarton, M. 'Gloves off at Paternoster; Attention to Detail in St. Paul's Proposal' *Building Design*, no. 912, Nov. 25 1988, pp 1, 10

Thalmann, N.M., Thalmann, D. 'Six Hundred References on Computer Animation' *The Journal of Visualisation and Computer Animation*, 1992, vol. 3, pp 147–74

Toy, M. *et al.* Editorial of 'Architects in Cyberspace II' *Architectural Design*, vol. 68, no. 11/12, 1998, p 7

Williams, A. 'Visualizing Architecture' *CADENCE*, May 2000

Winterkorn, E. 'How Important is IT to Architects?' *RIBA Journal*, vol. 107, no. 5, May 2000, pp 80–2

Wright, R. 'The Image in Art and "Computer Art"' *Leonardo, Computer Art in Context Supplement Issue*, 1989, pp 49–53

Architectural Design, XLIX (49), 10 November 1979, pp 1–32

Architectural Design, vol. 68, no. 11/12, Nov/Dec 1998, p 7

Architects' Journal
   vol. 155, no. 12, 22 March 1972, pp 590–603, 605
   vol. 158, no. 34, 22 August 1973, p 409
   vol. 171, no. 17, 23 April 1980, pp 792–3
   vol. 171, no. 22, 28 May 1980, pp 1051–72
   vol. 176, no. 37, 15 September 1982 pp 60–3
   vol. 177, no. 1, 5 January 1983, p 4
   vol. 177, no. 5, 2 February 1983, p 17
   vol. 179, no. 18, 2 May 1984, p 28
   vol. 181, no. 15, 10 April 1985, p 22
   vol. 187, no. 19, 11 May 1988, pp 46–68
   vol. 195, no. 8, 26 February 1992, pp 26–35
   vol. 209, no. 23, 10 June 1999, p 5

Architectural Record
   vol. 176, no. 1, January 1988, pp 125–9
   vol. 182, no. 6, June 1994, pp 42–9

Architectural Review
   LX-L, October 1926, pp 175–9
   vol. 109, no. 649, January 1951, p 42
   vol. 109, no. 651, March 1951, pp 135–50
   vol. 138, no. 821, July 1965, pp 13–20

CLXXXIV, 1039, September 1983, pp 26–37

CLXXV, 1044, February 1984, pp 28–37

CXCIII, 1159, November 1993, pp 26–44

ArchitectureWeek, 'SIGGRAPH Presents the future of Computer Graphics' August 2000, p. N1.1

Building Design

'With a Helping Hand' 8 May 1998

'This Year's Models' 6 October 2000

CICA, Bulletin,

no. 29 March 1989, p 3

no. 37 March 1991, p 4

CICA, Software Directory, version 1.4, 1993

RIBA Journal, 'CAD – the way we are' vol. 103, no. 2, February 1996, pp 65–6

Virtual Reality World, vol. 2, no. 6, November/December 1994, pp. 58–64

Conferences

Achten, H. *et al.* 'Virtual Reality in the Design Studio' eCAADe17 *Architectural Computing from Turing to 2000*, pp 169–77, University of Liverpool, September 1999

Aizlewood, M.E., Littlefair, P.J. 'Daylight Prediction Methods: a Survey of their Use' Proceedings of *National Lighting Conference*, University of Bath, CIBSE, 1996

Asanowicz, A. 'Evolution of Computer Aided Design: Three Generations of CAD' eCAADe17 *Architectural Computing from Turing to 2000*, pp 51–7, University of Liverpool, September 1999

Brewster, A. 'Emerging patterns of speculative digital visualisation in architecture' Greenwich 2000: *Digital Creativity Symposium*, pp 251–4, The University of Greenwich, London, UK, 13–15 January 2000

Bridges, A. 'The Power of Suggestion' Greenwich 2000: *Digital Creativity Symposium* pp 533–8, The University of Greenwich, London, UK, 13–15 January 2000

Clayton, M.J., Vasquez de Velasco, G. 'Stumbling, Backtracking, and Leapfrogging: Two Decades of Introductory Architectural Computing' ECAADe17 *Architectural Computing from Turing to 2000*, p. 156, University of Liverpool, September 1999

Cullinan, E. 'Drawing Out a Building' *Drawing The Future Symposium*, University of Huddersfield, April 1998

Day, A. 'The Use of Urban Visualisation Models To Aid Public Participation in the Planning Process' *Informing Technologies for Construction, Civil Engineering and Transport*, Brunel/SERC, 1993

Emmel, P., Hersch, R.D. 'Colour Calibration for Colour Reproduction' ISCAS 2000 *IEEE International Symposium on Circuits and Systems*, Geneva, Switzerland, 28–31 May 2000

Fellows, R. 'Architecture and Architectural Drawing in England 1880–1914' *Drawing The Future Symposium*, University of Huddersfield, April 1998

Holmgren, S., Rüdiger, B. 'IT in Urban Regeneration Projects' ECAADe17 Architectural Computing from Turing to 2000, pp 708–13, University of Liverpool, September 1999

Knight, M., Brown, A. 'Working in Virtual Environments through Appropriate Physical Interfaces' ECAADe17 Architectural Computing from Turing to 2000, pp. 431–6, University of Liverpool, September 1999

Richardson, M. 'Soane and Gandy – Orthogonal Drawings versus the Picturesque' *Drawing The Future Symposium*, University of Huddersfield, April 1998

Sanchez, S. *et al.* 'Bilbao: The Revitalisation of a City' ECAADe17 Architectural Computing from Turing to 2000, pp. 694–9, University of Liverpool, September 1999

Szalapaj, P., Chang, D.C. 'Computer Architectural Representation' ECAADe17 Architectural Computing from Turing to 2000, p 387, University of Liverpool, September 1999

Tweed, C. 'Prescribing Designs' eCAADe17 Architectural Computing from Turing to 2000, pp 51–7, University of Liverpool, September 1999

Ward, G.J. 'The Radiance Lighting Simulation and Rendering System' *Computer Graphics Proceedings, Annual Conference Series*, ACM SIGGRAPH, 1994

Wedgwood, A. 'AW Pugin: Architect, Designer and Draughtsman' *Drawing The Future Symposium*, University of Huddersfield, April 1998

Catalogues

Centre Georges Pompidou: *Archigram Exhibition*, 1994

Coope, R. *Jacques Gentilhâtre* Catalogue of the Drawings Collection of the RIBA, Farnborough, Hants: Gregg International, 1972

Cox, I. *The South Bank Exhibition: Festival of Britain* London: HM Stationery Office, 1951

The Drawings Collection of the Royal Institute of British Architects

Dunnett, J., Stamp, G. *Works 1: Erno Goldfinger* Exhibition 2–25 June, London: Architectural Association, 1983

Gropius, I. *Walter Gropius: Buildings, Plans, Projects 1906–1969* Washington DC: International Exhibitions Foundation, 1972

Harris, J. *Heinz Gallery Inaugural Exhibition*, London: RIBA, 1972

Moore, R. *Terry Farrell in the Context of London* Exhibition Catalogue, Heinz Gallery, 14 May–13 June 1987

Peto, J., Loveday, D. (eds) *Modern Britain 1929–1939* Exhibition 20 January – 6 June, London: The Design Museum, 1999

Raeburn, M., Wilson, V. (eds) *Le Corbusier: Architect of the Century* A Centenary Exhibition organised by the Arts Council of Great Britain in collaboration with the Fondation Le Corbusier, Paris, London: Hayward Gallery, 5 March–7 June 1987

Richardson, M., Stevens, M. (eds) *John Soane Architect* London: Royal Academy of Arts, 11 September–3 December 1999

The Soane Gallery: Harris, J. *William Kent 1685–1748, A Poet on Paper* Exhibition Catalogue, The Soane Gallery, 1998

South Bank Centre: Kemp, M., Roberts, J., Steadman, P. *Leonardo Da Vinci* Catalogue from the Hayward Gallery London Exhibition 26 January–16 April 1989

Reports

CICA, *Making IT Work for Your Business: Architectural IT Usage and Training Requirements* CICA guidance document, Partners in Innovation Initiative, 2000

Fallon, K. *CAD for Principals Council Newsletter*, vol. 1. no. 1, Spring 2000

Latham, M. *Constructing the Team: Final Report of the Government/Industry Review of Procurement and Contractual Arrangements in the UK Construction Industry*, HMSO, 1994

Index